COLONIAL

New Hampshire

by James Playsted Wood

New Hampshire was founded with the intention of creating a vast estate in the New World for the British gentry who sent the first settlers. The province—it was never actually a colony—had to win its independence three times, twice from Massachusetts Bay, once from England. It was the first British possession in North America to declare its independence, and it cast the deciding vote in the adoption of the United States Constitution.

In between its founding and statehood, New Hampshire had a history of bloody Indian wars, rival land claims, and religious disputes. Caught up in these events were several family dynasties and many rugged individuals, among them scoundrels and opportunists as well as men of bravery and character.

There were the Mason family, who owned New Hampshire and lost it after 139 years of litigation, and the patrician Wentworth clan, starting with William, who held off the Indians at eighty, as well as Benning and John, who were governors. There were Robert Rogers, Ranger hero of the French and Indian War, failed hero of the Revolution, and John Stark, another Ranger, who fought at Bunker Hill and Bennington.

All of these men and many more come to life again in this lusty, absorbing account of a turbulent time.

COLONIAL

New Hampshire

James Playsted Wood

THOMAS NELSON INC.
Nashville / Camden / New York

Photographs courtesy of the New Hampshire Historical Society, with the exception of the following: pp. 80, 123, Strawbery Banke, Inc.; p. 98, Donald Galbraith; pp. 120, 121, Dartmouth College; p. 122, Phillips Exeter Academy. Permission is gratefully acknowledged.

Published in Nashville, Tennessee, by Thomas Nelson Inc. and simultaneously in Don Mills, Ontario, by Thomas Nelson & Sons (Canada) Limited. Manufactured in the United States of America.

First edition

Library of Congress Cataloging in Publication Data

Wood, James Playsted
Colonial New Hampshire.

(Colonial history series)
Bibliography: p.
SUMMARY: Traces the history of New Hampshire from its discovery and founding to its role in the Revolution and adoption of the Federal Constitution.
1. New Hampshire–History–Colonial period, ca. 1600–1775–Juvenile literature. [1. New Hampshire–History–Colonial period] I. Title.
F37.W66 1973 974.2'02 73–10086
ISBN 0–8407–6316–6 73–10270
ISBN 0–8407–6317–4 (lib. bdg.)

Acknowledgments

For their thoughtful assistance in selecting the illustrations for this book my sincere thanks go to James F. Page, director, and Mary M. Hartman, reference librarian, New Hampshire Historical Society; James L. Garvin, curator, Strawbery Banke, Inc.; Paul Sadler, Jr., director of publications, the Phillips Exeter Academy; Kenneth C. Cramer, archivist, and Janice A. Ouellette of the Archives Department, the Baker Memorial Library, Dartmouth College; Mrs. Orin N. Chadbourne, Jackson, New Hampshire; Donald Galbraith and Mrs. Phyllis Reed, Charlestown, New Hampshire.

J. P. W.

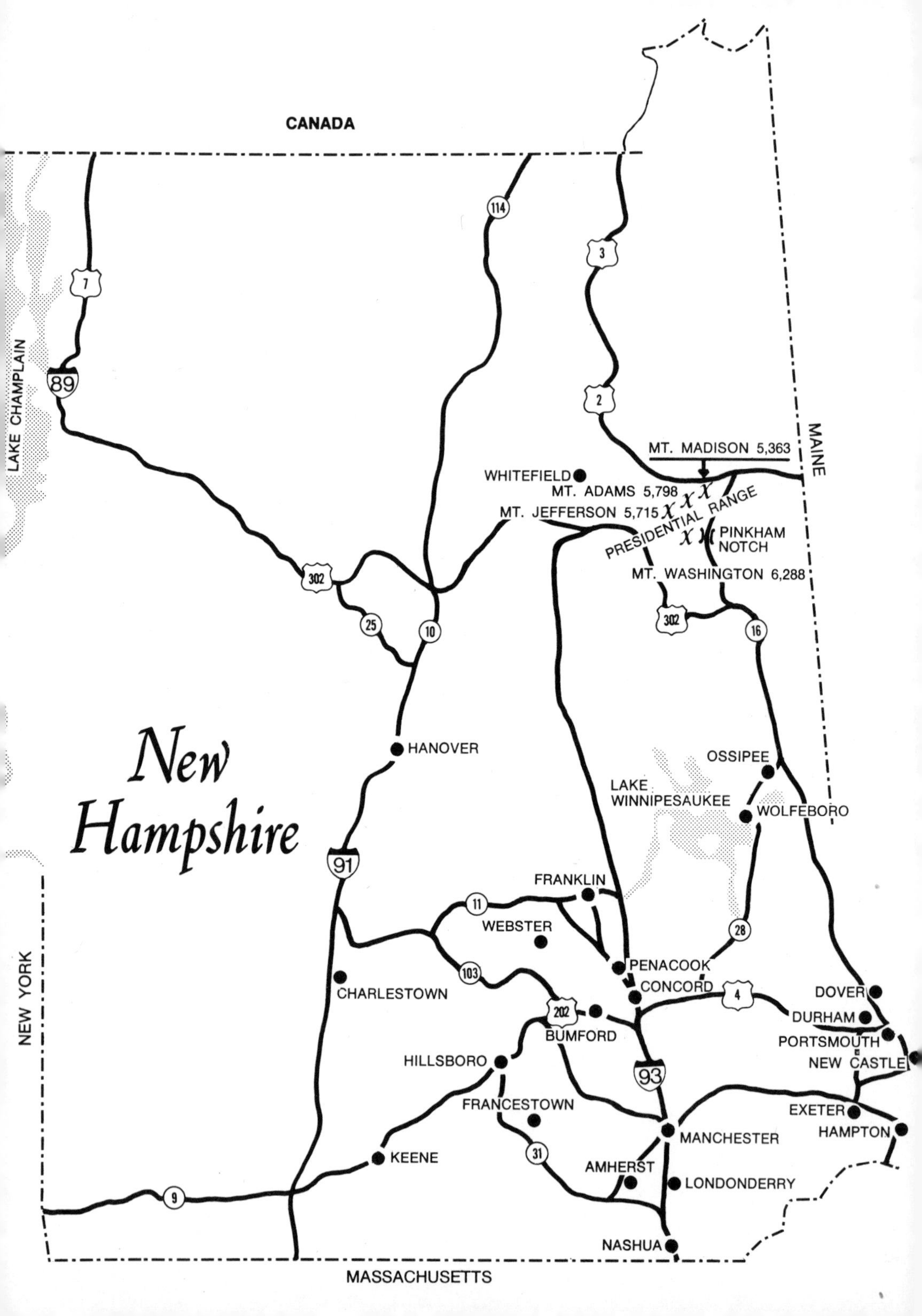
CANADA
LAKE CHAMPLAIN
MAINE
NEW YORK
MASSACHUSETTS
New Hampshire
114
3
7
89
2
MT. MADISON 5,363
WHITEFIELD
MT. ADAMS 5,798
MT. JEFFERSON 5,715
PRESIDENTIAL RANGE
PINKHAM NOTCH
MT. WASHINGTON 6,288
302
25
10
16
HANOVER
OSSIPEE
LAKE WINNIPESAUKEE
WOLFEBORO
91
FRANKLIN
11
WEBSTER
28
PENACOOK
103
CHARLESTOWN
CONCORD
4
DOVER
202
DURHAM
BUMFORD
PORTSMOUTH
HILLSBORO
93
NEW CASTLE
FRANCESTOWN
EXETER
MANCHESTER
HAMPTON
KEENE
31
AMHERST
LONDONDERRY
9
NASHUA

Contents

Papisseconewa, sagamore of the Pennacook tribe of New Hampshire.

CHAPTER ONE

Discovery and Founding

From the first, New Hampshire with its great natural beauty was different from the other New England colonies. In fact, it was not actually a colony, for it never had a colonial charter. Founded in 1623, only three years after the storied Pilgrims landed and began to build Plymouth Plantation, it was seven years older than Boston in Puritan Massachusetts Bay.

Unlike these settlements to the south, New Hampshire was not founded as a result of the religious disputes that were causing so much dissension in the sixteenth and seventeenth centuries. Instead, it was founded for commercial purposes, to be used as a vast landed estate in the New World for imaginative and strong-willed English gentlemen. From the beginning, New Hampshire was at once more aristocratic and more workaday plebeian than its neighbors.

New Hampshire had to win its independence not once but three times —twice from the predatory Massachusetts Bay colony, once from Great Britain. Generally it did not even wish for independence. There were sound practical reasons during its long early history why New Hampshire wished to be united and to stay united with the more populous and powerful Massachusetts Bay colony, and, long content under crown rule, New Hampshire was at first reluctant to separate from England, of which it considered itself a part. Yet it was the first of the British possessions in North America to declare its independence. Toughened in the long and bloody Indian wars, its troops fought hard and effectively during the American Revolution, and New Hampshire cast the deciding vote in the adoption of the United States constitution.

Again, in contrast to Massachusetts Bay, early New Hampshire was free of bigotry. Its people were decent, with a tolerant common sense. The hardheaded, hard-working, hard-living, hard-fighting New Hampshire men and women gave their province a character as distinct as its harsh northern climate and its varied terrain.

For geographically that part of the Northeast which became New Hampshire is varied too. It has a comparatively short stretch of the Atlantic coast, but inland are many lakes and rivers with their tributaries—rushing streams and torrential mountain flumes. In 700-square-mile Lake Winnipesaukee it has the largest inland body of water in New England, 500 feet above sea level. In the White Mountains of its north, Mount Washington, tallest mountain in the Northeast, pokes its head 6,300 feet into the clouds, its bare summit far above the timberline a forbidding height of high winds and vicious cold. About twenty of the other White Mountains are over 4,000 feet and thirty of them over 3,000. This region contains 1,400 square miles of rugged beauty, with passes or notches among the mountains and deep intervales of field and meadow where the gaps widen.

The average elevation in New Hampshire is 1,200 feet. The air is sharp and clear. In winter snow falls often and lies long—about 90 days of the year, in some places 120. There are about 160 days in the growing season in the southeast but only about 100 in the mountains. The seasons are sharply marked. In compensation for its winters, summer is brilliant and can seem tropical along the coast. In the mountains the fall coloring of the hardwoods against the dark pines, spruce, larch, and hemlock is breathtakingly beautiful.

Physically, New Hampshire is stimulating and demanding. It gives much, but it asked more in determination and sheer hardihood of its colonists than did milder Massachusetts Bay and still softer Connecticut.

Landfall

England based her claims to New England on the discoveries, maps, and reports of John Cabot, who reached Newfoundland in 1497 and sailed south as far as the 38th parallel of latitude, just as France based her claims to New France on the explorations of Samuel de Champlain, who about a hundred years later explored the Gulf of the St. Lawrence and sailed up the river as far as Lachine Falls. Even before Cabot, ships from various European nations had been coming each year to fish off the Newfoundland banks. After Cabot some ventured south to fish along the New England coast and to trade with the Indians, but no settlements were attempted at that time.

In 1603 Martin Pring, in command of the *Speedwell* and the *Discoverer,* sailed along the New Hampshire coast and entered the mouth of the Piscataqua River (then called Pascataqua, "the place of many deer") in search of sassafras, which was valued in Europe for its medicinal properties. Finding none, he went on down into Cape Cod Bay and landed at what later became Plymouth. There, the Indians watching, he built a barricaded tower, posted sentinals and two great mastiffs as guards, and stayed for seven weeks while his men cut and loaded sassafras. Pring described the Piscataqua region in his account of the New England coast from Casco Bay to Cape Cod, which was published in England on his return. In 1605 Champlain discovered the Isles of Shoals and also sailed down the New Hampshire coast.

Captain John Smith

Already a veteran soldier, mariner, and adventurer—leader of the Virginia Company's colony and hero of the Pocahontas legend—Captain John Smith explored and mapped the New England coast in 1614. With two ships Smith traced the Maine and New Hampshire coasts, where for years European vessels had fished and traded for furs with the Indians but had not ventured to land. He sailed into the wide harbor where the Piscataqua River flows into the Atlantic. Leaving his lieutenant, Thomas Hunt, in charge of the sister ship, Smith returned to England and in 1616 published his *Description of New England.*

Smith's account of the region he had named was the most complete and his map the most useful that had been produced up to that time. These and his urging of colonization for this part of the New World fired the imagination of many. He had brought back a shipload of furs and fish to support his words, and they were convincing evidence. Captain John Smith was particularly enthusiastic about what would be New Hampshire. He described the good harbor at the Piscataqua and praised the country inland.

In his *Description* Smith kept insisting that there was more wealth to be obtained from fishing in New England waters than from all the gold London adventurers had expected to find in Virginia. Of New Hampshire he wrote:

> Here should be no hard landlords to rack us with high rents, or extorted fines to consume us; here every man may be master and owner of his labor and land in a short time. . . . The sea there near the Isle of Shoals is the strangest fish-pond I ever saw. What sport doth yield a more pleasing content, and less hurt or charge, than angling with a hook, and crossing the sweet air from isle to isle over the silent streams of a calm sea?

Sir Ferdinando Gorges

If Captain John Smith had his visions of what northern New England was and could become, so did others more highly placed than he, men in position to try to make their dreams reality.

One such man was Ferdinando Gorges. Born in 1566, he had been at the court of Queen Elizabeth as a young man and a companion of Sir Walter Raleigh. At twenty-three he was captured by a ship of the Spanish Armada, but by 1589 he was in command of troops fighting for Henry IV of France and had distinguished himself at the siege of Rouen. For this service he was later knighted. In 1596, Gorges was made captain of the fort at Plymouth, England, and of St. Nicholas Isle. The next year he went with Essex on his expedition to the Azores, but except for one short interruption, he kept his Plymouth post until 1629.

Greatly interested in the colonization of America, Gorges became a member of the Plymouth Company in 1606. He sent out ships to fish and trade, and it was he who hired Captain John Smith to make his 1614 voyage and others in an attempt to settle the area. One of Smith's ships, after a search for the fabled Northwest Passage to the Indies, brought five Indians back to England. Gorges took three of them, Manida, Skettwarroes, and Tasquantum, and listened closely as they described their tribes and leaders and told about the Indian way of life and mode of warfare. He also had the Indians make outline maps of the mountains and rivers they knew.

In 1620 Gorges persuaded the English king to form the Council for New England "for the planting, ruling, and governing of New England in America." This body was made up of forty noblemen, among them the Dukes of Lennox, Buckingham, and Hamilton, and the Marquises of Pembroke, Arundel, Bath, Southampton, Salisbury, and Warwick. Leader in the Plymouth Council was Sir Ferdinando Gorges.

Gorges had tried unsuccessfully to establish an English colony at the mouth of the Kennebec in 1607; thirty years later he became Lord Proprietor of the whole of Maine.

Captain John Mason

John Mason was born in 1586 in King's Lynn, Norfolk, a busy port on the Ouse, its wharves and exchanges crowded with shipmasters and sailors who knew distant parts of the known world. Mason is thought to have attended Magdalen College, Oxford, matriculating on June 25, 1602, when he was fifteen years of age. The youth later took to the sea, and in 1610 was sent in command of two English warships and two pinnaces to subdue the Hebrides and bring them under Scottish law. At twenty Mason married Anne Greene, daughter of a London goldsmith. They had one child. In 1615 Captain Mason was appointed governor of an English colony in Newfoundland.

Newfoundland was already a busy place. Thousands of British seamen were there during the fishing season and men from ships of other nations. There were continual disputes in the courts. Mason was enthralled by Newfoundland, and he spent the next six years there.

Several new plantations were founded during his governorship. Enthusiasm for colonization was at its height, and Captain John Mason was one of the most enthusiastic for the settlement both of Newfoundland and of the New England land to the south. He may have seen parts of it because, being an able and conscientious governor, he was also King's lieutenant in command of British ships sent to battle the pirates who already infested the waters of Newfoundland and New England.

Mason thoroughly explored and mapped Newfoundland. He described its climate, vegetation, minerals, fauna, and particularly its fishing waters. Like Captain John Smith, he was convinced of the wealth to be obtained in the fisheries; unlike Smith, he saw the actual fishing. In *A Brief Discourse of the New-Found-land*, published in Edinburgh in 1620, he wrote of the herring, smelt, and salmon, and spoke of

> cods so thick by the shore that we hardly have been able to row a boat through them. I have killed of them with a pike. Of these, three men to sea in a boat with some on shore to dress and dry them in 30 days will kill betwixt 25 and thirty thousand, worth with the oil arising in them 100 or 120 pound. . . . What should I speak of Whales called Gibberts, Dogfish, Porpoises, Hering-Hogges, Squides a rare kinde of fish at his mouth squirting mattere forth like Inke, Flownders, Crabbes, Cunners, Catfish, Millers, Thunnes, etc. of al which there are innumerable in the Summer season; likewise of Lobsters plentie . . . now of shell fish there is Scalupes, Musseles, Urenas, Hens, Periwinckles, &c.

Mason pointed out that Newfoundland was near England, calling it halfway to Virginia, and he urged colonization there at the going rate of ten shillings for a man's passage and twenty shillings for his food, far less than it cost to send a settler to Virginia or Bermuda.

Mason meant what he said, and as soon as he returned to England, he did something about it. Presumably he already knew Sir Ferdinando Gorges. Quickly they were at work together in the Council for New England at Plymouth.

In 1622, the year after Mason's return from Newfoundland, he and Gorges joined forces in obtaining from the Council for New England a series of land grants in what became Maine and New Hampshire. One grant to Mason was for the region between the Salem and Merrimack Rivers, which was to be called Marianna. Another grant, given

Mason and Gorges jointly, was for the region between the Merrimack and Kennebec Rivers for sixty miles inland. To the Laconia Company —which was Mason, Gorges, and a few mercantile adventurers—was granted a large territory around the Lake of the Iroquois (Lake Champlain), together with a thousand acres of seacoast at the point to be selected.

To Captain John Mason alone was granted, on November 6, 1629, the land between the Merrimack and Piscataqua Rivers, and to this, after his home county in England, he gave the name "New Hampshire." The Pescataway Grant gave Mason and his associates the Isles of Shoals and the land on both sides of the Piscataqua extending west thirty miles from the coast. Before the Council for New England was dissolved in 1635, Mason had been granted additional contiguous land under the New Hampshire name.

The Plan

Both Captain John Mason and Sir Ferdinando Gorges were adventurous men of action. Wealthy and well placed, they were also substantial members of England's ruling class. Naturally they expected to extend to their crown-granted lands in America the kind of life they knew and understood in the Old World. To them New England across the Atlantic Ocean would be but a removed part of Old England. As lords of the manor, they and their kinsmen would possess and govern land worked by tenant farmers and enjoy the rewards of the industry of their village tradesmen and artisans. They hoped for great riches from furs, lumber, and fish, even for the discovery of valuable minerals, said to exist in Laconia, but they were not speculators or even impatient. They risked much and they expected to gain much, but Mason in particular knew it might take time.

In the eyes of England, Plymouth Plantation was the refuge of religious eccentrics whose Separatist determination had driven them first to Holland, then to America. Its people were exiles. These Puritan fanatics, many of them gentlemen of wealth and learning, had either disapproved of the Church of England or had been unable to obtain political preferment under the Stuarts–sometimes both. As intolerant as they were courageous, the Puritans were defiant exiles too. Massachusetts Bay was to be their New Jerusalem. Taking their own strong charter with them, they set up there a Holy Commonwealth that was almost an independent religious, social, and political entity.

New Hampshire, on the other hand, was colonized under English gentlemen whose rights and privileges had been granted by the court. Both Gorges and Mason were staunch Church of England men. The first settlers they sent to New Hampshire understood life as they understood it. They were not rebels against either the crown or the church but were Englishmen who expected to be ruled (and cared for) by English gentlemen. If they were religious at all, they remained devoted to the established church of their native country.

The First Settlements in New Hampshire

In the early spring of 1623 Mason and Gorges began to send colonists to their domain. Gorges described it thus:

> A faire large river, well replenisht with many fruitfull islands; the ayre thereof is pure and wholesome; the country pleasant, having some high hills of goodly forrests and faire vallies and plaines fruitfull in corn, vines, chesnuts, wall nuts, and infinite sorts of other fruits, large rivers well stored with fish, and invironed with goodly meadows full of timber trees.

In 1623 David Thomson, a Scot described as a scholar and traveler, led the first group of settlers to six thousand acres evidently acquired through arrangement with Captain Mason, for by his deeds from King James I, Mason had power over all lands and water, forests, mines, and fisheries and was enjoined to found churches "to be dedicated or consecrated according to the ecclesiastical laws of England." Thomson headed a fishing and trading group organized to operate for five years. They settled near the mouth of the Piscataqua and built a house there. At first called Pannaway, then Pescataway, it became Little Harbour,
 then Strawbery Banke, finally Portsmouth. The settlement was made

on about five hundred acres of a peninsula called Odiorne's Point, which had a hill for lookout and could be fortified for defense.

With Thomson came William and Edward Hilton, fishmongers of London. The Hiltons and their followers went a few miles farther up the Piscataqua and established a settlement at Dover Point, which was at first called Newichwanack and ultimately became Dover.

The proprietors kept their people–stewards or factors and "servants" or employees–well supplied with arms and ammunition, tools, provisions, clothing, and other necessities. Thus they did not suffer the hardships, so often recounted, that the Pilgrims endured during their first year at Plymouth or that the Puritans who came first to Salem in 1629 knew.

In the spring of 1630 the Laconia Company sent the 80-ton, 10-gun bark *Warwick* with more settlers, among them Captain Walter Neale (though some accounts place him in New Hampshire earlier), Ambrose Gibbons, Thomas Wonerton, Henry Jocelyn, Francis Norton, and Samson Lane (all stewards); Reginald Furnald, the doctor (chirurgeon); Thomas Chateron, Ralph and Henry Gee, George Vaughan; and three Chadbournes, Humphrey, William, and William, Jr. Humphrey Chadbourne is said to have built the Great House at Strawbery Banke that Captain Mason referred to as his manor. Mason and Gorges sent more than sixty men to the New Hampshire settlements. They also sent twenty-two women, as well as eight Danes to build sawmills and make potash, but none of their names are known.

The Laconia Company then sent another vessel, the *Pied Cow*, with materials for their people. Both the *Warwick* and the *Pied Cow* seem to have made more voyages across the Atlantic from England, returning from the Piscataqua loaded with furs, fish, and lumber.

It is said that David Thomson, becoming dissatisfied with his agreement with Mason and Gorges, left after a year and went to live on an island in Boston Harbor. Other of the often contradictory accounts say that he remained at Strawbery Banke for three years. At any rate, he was succeeded by Neale, who seems to have had some kind of partnership with the proprietors. Because Neale was in charge at Strawbery

Banke (or Portsmouth) and reported to Mason, he has been called the first governor of New Hampshire.

At the same time Ambrose Wiggin, representing the Gorges interests, was in charge of the upper plantation at Dover Point. Wiggin and Neale got into a dispute as to which settlement owned a point of land, and combat threatened. The problem was settled without recourse to arms, but after that the place became known as Bloody Point. Undoubtedly there were other disputes, but most of the time the settlers were too busy to quarrel. They cleared the land and built their log houses. They put up sawmills to provide lumber for better houses and for shipping to England. They built salt mills to furnish salt for packing the fish they caught and shipped out of the Piscataqua. They traded trinkets and company goods with the Indians for precious furs.

The Indians

When the settlers arrived at Plymouth in 1620, they were surprised not to find the hordes of Indians that Captain John Smith had reported in New England. Later they discovered that in 1617 the bubonic plague had killed off more than half of the natives between the Penobscot River and Narragansett Bay. The Indians in New Hampshire suffered along with the rest, but George Barstow in his *History of New Hampshire* (1842) says there were about five thousand of them—although who could have taken the census and how, it is difficult to imagine. There was a small tribe at Dover and another small tribe at what became Exeter. Algonquins all, there were the Ossipees, the Winnipisseockeege, the Pequawket, and the Pennacook, the general name of these federated tribes in New Hampshire being the Pawtuckets. There were also the warlike Abnaki.

The Indians were friendly at first. Though Thomas Hunt had treacherously abducted twenty of them and sold them into slavery in Spain—an act which his commander, Captain John Smith, and many others condemned—the Indians had not yet learned to fear and hate the white

 men and their ways. It is safe to assume that curious Indians frequented both Portsmouth and Dover early and were anxious to trade their beaver pelts for clothes and tools, but there was one dark omen of the not far distant time when the Indians would not be friendly at all. In 1628 the New Hampshire settlers were unhappily surprised to find Indians hunting with guns near Dover. The sale of firearms to Indians was strictly forbidden, but the Indians had obtained them from a greedy and conscienceless trader at Weymouth in Massachusetts Bay.

Portsmouth and Dover were becoming firmly established, but Captain Mason and his fellow investors were reaping little profit from their considerable outlay. Level-headed as well as generous, Mason was deeply interested in his New Hampshire. He sent his people specially selected Danish cattle of a large, yellowish breed, and they thrived and increased. He kept in constant touch with his stewards and kept his people well supplied, but the Laconia Company was beginning to expect some return. They looked to the interior of the north and west of New Hampshire for some of the mineral wealth the province was fabled to contain.

Exploration

Captain Walter Neale was a professional soldier and an adventurer like Sir Walter Raleigh and Captain John Smith. In charge of the fishing and salt making at Portsmouth, he also drilled the New Hampshire men in arms and planned the fortification of what for many years was called "the Bank." He knew how, for between adventures Neale had been captain and drill master of the London militia.

In 1632 Neale and two other hardy explorers, Darby Field and Henry Jocelyn, set out on foot for country they thought was less than a hundred miles away. Their mission was to discover gold and precious stones and to establish a fur trade with the Indians of the interior. The three men fought their way through the wilderness for days to the land of mountains and lakes. They had reached the White Mountains —much farther away than they had expected—and believed they were within one more day's journey of their ultimate destination when they were forced back by lack of provisions.

The men found no gold or other treasure, only some crystals for which they named the White Mountains the Crystal Hills, and even the crystals proved worthless.

Like all travelers, however, they brought back wondrous tales of the marvels they had seen. The White Mountains were a ridge of 300 miles (100 leagues), covered with snow throughout the year. On one mountain was a treeless, mossy plain that took a day's journey to traverse. At the end of it was a pile of stones forming a rocky stairway a mile high, which ascended into the clouds. There was a clear lake at its summit, and beyond that was a land of rocky hills and dark forest.

Not even the Indians knew this wonderful country. They called the White Mountains Agiocochook and venerated their great heights. They never climbed the mountains, for they believed spirits guarded the cliffs and waterfalls and that the Great Spirit hovered above them in the mountain clouds.

No sooner had Neale returned to Portsmouth than he sailed, in command of four small ships with forty men from the upper and lower plantations and twenty more men from Boston, in pursuit of the pirate Dixie Bull, who was harassing shipping off the coast. They did not catch him, but before they returned they hanged an Indian who had murdered a white man.

In 1634 Gorges and Mason divided their huge holdings. Gorges took the territory east of the Piscataqua, which became Maine, while Mason took the land west of the river, which was New Hampshire. *Hampshire* derives from the Anglo-Saxon *Hamtunscir, ham* meaning home and *tun* a garden, while *scir* is a shire or county. The whole means a permanent dwelling place. Thus New Hampshire was home in America.

In May 1634 Mason wrote his factor:

> The servants with you, and such others as remain upon the company's charge, are to be discharged and paid their wages out of the stock of beaver in your hands, at the rate of 12 shillings the pound. And you must afford my people some house-room at Newichwannock house; and the cows and goats, which are all mine, and 14 swine with their in-

> crease, some place grounds to be upon till we have some place provided upon my new-divided lands. The chrystal stones you sent are of little or no value. . . . Good iron or lead ore I should like better of, if it could be found. I have disbursed a great deal of money in the plantation and never received one penny; but hope, if there were once a discovery of the lakes, that I should, in some reasonable time be reimbursed again.

Mason's Investment

Mason spent a total of £22,000 sterling, a vast sum in the early seventeenth century, in settling and trying to develop New Hampshire. As his grants had enjoined, his people had all the rights and privileges of Englishmen at home. They could import and export from the Piscataqua without restriction. They were well supplied with everything they could conceivably need. An inventory of the goods at the Piscataqua in July 1635 showed quantities of clothes, food, tools, weapons, and ammunition on hand.

A long list of stores had in it 50 cloth cassocks and breeches, 150 canvas cassocks and breeches, 80 shirts, 58 hats, 130 pairs of shoes, 204 pairs of stockings. There were caps, cloth, and hides. There was, of course, plenty of wine and aqua vitae (whiskey) and tobacco. The settlements had 6 "great shallops" (open boats with sails), 5 fishing boats with sails, all of them with anchors, cables, and rigging, and 13 skiffs. Piscataqua had in stock 140 bushels of corn, 8 barrels of oatmeal, 32 barrels of meat, 29 barrels of butt malt, 153 pounds of peas, 610 candles, and 1,512 pounds of sugar.

Physically Mason's people in New Hampshire were well cared for, and he had made provision for their spiritual welfare in the Church of England. Piscataqua had one Great Bible, twelve service books, one pewter flagon, one Communion cup and cover of silver, a fine tablecloth, and two napkins.

Mason's Death

When he was made vice admiral of New England in 1635, Captain John Mason was still sanguine and still deeply concerned about the welfare of his people. He said that New England was large and spacious and that it had thirteen thousand English inhabitants with about forty ships along three hundred miles of coast. He was preparing to visit New Hampshire when he died in December of that same year.

The will of the man who had been governor of Portsmouth in England, treasurer and paymaster of the royal army, and active member of the Council of New England bequeathed New Hampshire to his grandchildren, the oldest of whom was only seven at the time. It directed that his widow and brother-in-law, Sir John Wollaston, give 1,000 acres "in my county of New Hampshire or Manor of Mason Hall" for a church and another 1,000 acres for a grammar school at some convenient place in New Hampshire. Mason left 2,000 acres to his native King's Lynn. None of these bequests were ever fulfilled, for unintentionally Mason left New Hampshire a difficult problem. Cessation of his support left the Piscataqua plantation in straits. Claims of the Mason heirs resulted in conflict and long-drawn-out litigation for nearly a hundred years.

As a loyal servant of England, a devout Anglican, and a man of wide accomplishments, naval, military, and civilian, Captain John Mason was buried in Westminster Abbey. Puritan Massachusetts Bay was delighted —not at the posthumous honor accorded the founder of New Hampshire but at his removal.

Under its liberal interpretation of the charter granted the Governor and Company of the Massachusetts Bay in New England in 1628, the colony of Massachusetts now ignored the grants to Gorges and Mason. It insisted that it owned everything to three miles north of the *source* of the Merrimack River, thus almost all of Maine and New Hampshire. The Bay authorities had another reason for rejoicing. John Mason had been a staunch adherent of the Church of England, and the Puritans feared his bringing the institution they detested into New England. In Mason's death the Puritans saw another sign of God's favor to their Holy Commonwealth.

CHAPTER TWO

The Four Towns

Finding no income from heavy outgo, Mrs. Anne Mason ceased to send supplies to New Hampshire or remittances to the Mason agents and tenants. This distressed some people in the colony but simplified matters for others. They merely laid claim to the land and to the houses they had built, and divided Captain Mason's possessions among themselves. Walter Neale had returned to England and been succeeded by Francis Williams. When Thomas Warnerton, who followed them as steward, quit the Great House, he shipped the goods and arms that had belonged to Mason to Port Royal, where he sold them to the French. Another man did well too. He drove a hundred Mason-owned oxen to Boston and sold them there for £20 sterling a head. He did not return to New Hampshire but settled at Charlestown near Boston.

Portsmouth

Thomas Wiggin was sent to England to seek other support for Portsmouth. He seems not to have obtained new financial backing, but he did succeed in getting some west-of-England families of substance to emigrate to the Piscataqua.

Portsmouth, as Exeter, Hampton, and Dover did, had established a town government of its own. Its freemen had elected Francis Williams governor and Ambrose Gibbons and Thomas Warnerton assistants. On May 25, 1640, the people of Portsmouth deeded fifty acres of land around the chapel and parsonage they had built as glebe land for the church, which would thus be endowed, after the English fashion, with any profit accruing from it.

Furnishing the chapel with the ecclestical service sent by Mason, they brought the Reverend Richard Gibson, an Anglican clergyman, from England to be their first rector. Almost immediately, Massachusetts Bay, which had no actual jurisdiction at that time, haled him before its court for violating Puritan forms of worship—"scandalizing the government and denying their title." They dismissed Gibson but did not punish him because he left the country. The Portsmouth church then had no regular minister until the appointment of the Reverend Joshua Moody in 1658.

Hampton

The General Court of Massachusetts made its presence felt in New Hampshire in a different way. Acting on its claim of ownership to the lower part of New Hampshire, it had a blockhouse built there in 1635. In 1638 it gave a grant of land at Winnicummet to the Reverend Stephen Bachiler, an Oxford graduate and Puritan minister, and his congregation. They sailed up the Winnicummet River in shallops to take possession, and were later joined by more Puritans who came from Norfolk in England. The next year they changed the name of the place to Hampton and established the new settlement under the laws of Massachusetts Bay as well as some of their own.

Conservation was practiced early in New Hampshire. By English law every tree of twenty-four inches or more in diameter belonged to the king. For well over a century New England supplied the best white pine masts for the British navy. Hampton passed additional forestry laws. It elected three woodwards in 1639. Without their permission no man could fell a tree except on his own lot. The fine was ten shillings for every tree illegally cut down. Sometimes trees were assigned to a man, but he had to cut them down within a month and make use of them within three months; otherwise, the trees were at the disposal of the town woodwards.

Hampton held frequent town meetings in which the entire body of freemen decided on town actions. When this method became too cumbersome, seven selectmen were elected, the number later reduced to five.

Their stated duty consisted of "managing the prudential affairs" of the town.

Hampton even instituted wage controls. In 1644 the town passed a regulation under which workmen were allowed one shilling and fourpence a day from September through March, and one shilling and eightpence from March to September. For mowing—hard work with hand scythes—men were to be paid two shillings a day at any time. A day's work with four oxen and a cart was five or six shillings, depending on the season. Hampton later voted that even the best workmen could not receive more than two shillings a day while the others got no more than one shilling and eightpence.

Exeter

Without intending to, Massachusetts Bay effected the founding of another New Hampshire town.

When it became annoyed with people it did not like—Quakers, Anabaptists, and others whose religious opinions differed in any way from its own—Massachusetts Bay usually hanged them or banished them. In 1635 Mrs. Anne Hutchinson began to preach in Boston that the true Christian comes to God through his own indwelling spirit, not through obeying the laws of the Puritan Church as taught by its ministers and enforced by the Massachusetts magistrates. For this, Mrs. Hutchinson was tried for heresy, convicted and excommunicated. Her soul was formally given up to the Devil, and she was banished. Anne Hutchinson and her family took refuge in Rhode Island.

Her brother-in-law, the Reverend John Wheelwright, husband of her sister Mary, likewise proved obnoxious to the ministers of Boston and the authorities of Massachusetts Bay. Like his sister-in-law, he was an antinomian. Ironically, he found the Boston Puritans too liberal. The question was theological and so abstruse that even Governor John Winthrop was unsure he knew all that was implied, but it was enough that Wheelwright defied Puritan doctrine and practice in Boston. Specifically, Wheelwright, a graduate of Sidney College, Cambridge, and an ordained priest of the Church of England, held to the strict Calvinistic tenet of predestination. This means that God elects to grace and eternal bliss those whom He pleases, and discards all others. Boston had relaxed so far as to preach and urge the practice of attaining salvation by good works—that is, getting to heaven by being good.

On a fast day in 1637 Wheelwright spoke out against this laxity. In consequence, he was brought up on charges. When he refused to retract, he was disenfranchised and banished from Massachusetts Bay for sedition and contempt of the civil authorities.

Wheelwright, with his family and friends and those of his Boston congregation who shared his views, then moved to New Hampshire and founded Exeter on land which Wheelwright claimed he had bought from the Indians in 1629.

The validity of his deed was questioned even in colonial times, when it was regarded by some as a clever forgery. Cotton Mather himself, when questioned as to its authenticity, expressed doubts. Legitimate or illegitimate, this deed, signed with the marks of Passaconaway, Runaawitt, Whangnonawitt, and Rowls, sagamores respectively of the Pennacook, Pentucket, Squamscot, and Newichawanoc tribes, gave all rights to some twenty square miles to John Wheelwright, Augustus Storer, Thomas Wight, William Wentworth, Thomas Levett, "and their heirs forever."

The Exeter deed with its many and detailed clauses said that it was granted by the sagamores so that their tribes would be strengthened against their enemies the Tarateens (Abnaki), and was given for "a competent valuation in goods already received in coats, shirts and kettles." The English witnesses were the original great men of New Hampshire: Walter Neale, governor; George Vaughan, factor; Ambrose Gibbons, trader; and (for the company of Laconia) Richard Vines, governor; Richard Bennington, assistant; Thomas Wiggin, agent; and Edward Hilton, steward of the plantation at Hilton's Point.

The Exeter Combination

As soon as they reached their new home the banished antinomians drew up the Exeter Agreement. Signed by Wheelwright and thirty-six other men, it was a voluntary association of the people to live together in peace under their own rules. A church and state covenant, it has been lauded as the first institution of independent government in New Hampshire.

> Whereas it hath pleased the Lord to move the heart of our dread sovereign Charles, by the grace of God, king, &c, to grant license and libertye to sundry of his subjects to plant themselves in the westerne parts of America. We his loyal subjects brethren of the church in Exeter, situate and lying upon the river Pascataqua, with other inhabitants there, considering with ourselves the holy will of God and our own necessity, that we should not live without wholsom laws and civil government among us, of which we are altogether destitute; do in the name of Christ and in the sight of God, combine ourselves together to erect and set up among us such government as shall be to our best discerning agreeable to the will of God, professing ourselves subjects to our sovereign lord king Charles according to the libertyes of our English colony of Massachusetts, and binding of ourselves solemnly by the grace and help of Christ, and in his name and fear to submit ourselves to such godly and christian lawes as are established in the realm of England to our best knowledge, and to all other such laws which shall upon good grounds be made and enacted among us according to God, that we may live quietly and peaceably together in all godliness and honesty. Mo.8, d.4.1639, as attests our hands.

Dover

Exeter chose its rulers and assistants annually, and the people were sworn to obey them in this first "combination" or "association." Hampton and Exeter were Puritan settlements. The older Portsmouth and Dover were not. There were formal protestations of loyalty to England in the Exeter agreement, but a real feeling of loyalty existed in Portsmouth and Dover, which were more tolerant and, at least nominally, Church of England. They felt themselves to be directly responsible to and under the protection of England. Both towns soon drew up agreements patterned after the Exeter Combination, but they included no excessive piety or acknowledgment of Massachusetts.

The shorter and simpler Dover Agreement of October 22, 1640, said:

> Whereas sundry mischiefes and inconveniences have befallen us, and more and greater may be in regard of want of civill Government, his Gratious Maie [Majesty] having hitherto settled no order for us to our knowledge.
>
> Wee whose names are underwritten being Inhabitants upon the River Pasataquack have voluntarily agreed to combine ourselves into a body politique that wee may the more comfortably enjoy the benefits of his Maties [Majesty's] law together with all such orders as shall be concluded by a major part of the Freemen of our Society in case they bee not repugnant to the lawes of England and administered in behalfe of his Majesty. . . .

Dover sounds a little tentative, a little lost, without the direction and protection of John Mason. It lacked Exeter's Puritan self-assurance and Wheelwright's clerical wordiness. It had also suffered severe disturbance.

Church Controversy

The "heresy" that had led to the founding of Exeter had infected Dover as well. Governor John Winthrop had imported a Captain John Underhill, veteran of army service in the Netherlands, to train the Massachusetts Bay people in arms, but Underhill had proved too outspoken. Siding with John Wheelwright, he complained of the arbitrariness of the ministers and magistrates in Boston. The Puritans did not brook such criticism. They banished Underhill, who then came to Dover and, although Winthrop wrote warning of his heretical opinions and immoral behavior, he was somehow elected governor.

Underhill busied himself with establishing a church in Dover and then used his influence to have Hanserd Knollys, an Anabaptist who had come over the year before, made its minister, even though Knollys had been forbidden to preach in New Hampshire.

Massachusetts Bay continued its warnings and threatened to move against Underhill and Knollys, but leaders in both Portsmouth and Dover asked that it not interfere. Tactfully, Knollys went to Boston and made public confession of assorted sins before the assembled ministers and magistrates. Accused, like Knollys, of sexual immorality as well as heresy, Underhill also confessed, but lost. He was excommunicated. He was enraged when on his return to New Hampshire he found that he had been dismissed as governor in Dover.

Religion was a serious matter at that time, and religious disputes aroused fierce partisanships. The Dover controversy was shot full of piety and skulduggery, but it also had overtones of comedy. It grew more involved when another minister, Thomas Larkham, fled Boston, came to Dover, and began to preach in opposition to Knollys. After the Puritan manner, Larkham tried to assume civil as well as ecclesiastical rule. This was too much. Dover's more influential people restored Knollys to their pulpit, and Knollys promptly excommunicated Larkham.

Riot

The result was a farcical riot. Larkham snatched Knollys's hat from his head, claiming he had not paid for it. The Dover magistrates then summoned Underhill to answer various charges. Instead, Underhill collected his forces, including the Reverend Knollys, who armed himself with a pistol, and another enthusiast who marched with a Bible hoisted on his halberd.

At this juncture the Larkham forces, declining armed combat, sent downriver asking the aid of Governor Williams of Portsmouth. Williams promptly sailed to Dover with an armed force.

The Portsmouth men besieged Knollys's house, in which Underhill, too, had taken sanctuary, and guarded it day and night until a court could be convened. Then, with Governor Williams sitting as judge, Captain Underhill and his troops were convicted of causing a riot and were fined and banished from the Piscataqua.

One charge that led to Underhill's conviction was that he had secretly been trying to persuade Dover's people to ally themselves with Massachusetts Bay in order to ingratiate himself there. Perhaps he had been, for when the convicted rioters appealed to Boston, Massachusetts Bay sent a commission of ministers and magistrates, led by Simon Bradstreet, to inquire into the fracas. They trudged on foot the more than sixty miles to Dover, found both sides at fault, and revoked both the excommunication of Larkham and the fines and banishment imposed on Captain John Underhill and the Reverend Hanserd Knollys. Knollys was then convicted of immoral behavior and returned to England, where he got into further ministerial difficulties. They could not have disturbed him too much, for he lived to be ninety-three years old.

In Boston Captain Underhill made another public confession of the error of his ways and was restored to favor, but then he left for New York and took a military command under the Dutch. With a company of 120 men he acquitted himself laudably there, being credited with a total kill of 450 Indians.

Situation of New Hampshire

The four New Hampshire towns stood alone. As a part of Massachusetts Bay, which it considered itself, Hampton had some military protection. Portsmouth, Dover, and Exeter had none. Each was an independent, self-governing community. New Hampshire had no central authority or any existence as a social and political unit. There was virtue in this system of voluntary local associations, but there was also danger.

The New York Dutch pressed New England from the south, the French in Canada from the north. There was always danger of Indian attack. Plymouth Plantation lost its charter, the crown demanding its surrender because it was being used for private gain rather than for the spread of religion and the good of England. Plymouth was under the sway of Massachusetts Bay.

England was far too distraught now with the civil war which would lead to Cromwell's victories, the execution of Charles I, and the establishment of the Commonwealth to pay much attention to her North American colonies or to render them assistance. When the Puritans came to power in England, Massachusetts Bay basked in favor. Populous and prosperous, it acted more and more like a sovereign state.

CHAPTER THREE

Union with Massachusettes Bay

Realization of their need for a stronger government and the protection it would afford led Portsmouth and Dover to petition Massachusetts Bay to take them under its protection. Rather reluctantly, Exeter followed. With its pious acquisitiveness Massachusetts Bay, which already controlled Hampton, was only too willing to agree.

The four towns were incorporated in Massachusetts in 1641, but retained their own town governments with their own courts, whose decisions in major cases were subject to superior Massachusetts judgments. The towns were allowed their existing fishing, lumbering, and planting privileges, and New Hampshire was granted two deputies to represent it in the Massachusetts General Court, which was really that colony's legislature. It is still so designated in the Commonwealth of Massachusetts.

Religious Toleration

As Larkham, like Knollys, had returned to England, Massachusetts Bay sent a minister of its own choosing to Dover. The union with Massachusetts also meant ministerial changes for Exeter and Hampton. The Reverend John Wheelwright had been banished from the Puritan colony, so he was forced to abdicate. He fled to Wells, Maine. In 1643 he was allowed to visit Boston and soon afterward found it convenient to repent, recant his antinomianism, and ask forgiveness and release from banishment. Pardon was granted, and in 1647, when Hampton's aged minister, Stephen Bachiler, went to Exeter, Wheelwright became pastor at Hampton.

When Oliver Cromwell took command as Lord Protector, Wheelwright returned to England. Cromwell, who had known him when they were both Cambridge undergraduates, welcomed him cordially, saying, "I remember the time when I have been more afraid of meeting Wheelwright at football than of meeting any army since in the field."

The Lord Protector appointed Wheelwright to a post of some importance in his government, and Wheelwright held it until the Restoration of the British monarchy in 1660. He then returned to New Hampshire.

New Hampshire gained one important concession from the Massachusetts General Court. In Massachusetts Bay only members of the established—that is, the Puritan or Congregational—Church were permitted to vote. Church membership, as a qualification for the franchise, was not required of New Hampshire freemen.

New Hampshire was subject now to the Puritan rule of Massachusetts Bay, but its fishermen, farmers, loggers, mechanics, and traders continued to go much their own way, seemingly with little interference from Boston. They were far enough away to escape some of the inquisitorial bigotry. Besides, they came of different English stock and were more tolerant, concerned less with Calvinistic theology and more with practical affairs.

A Massachusetts commission, sent soon after the union was effected, confirmed the chosen leaders of the New Hampshire towns in their offices. Some of them were men who had performed so well as Mason's agents that year after year they were elected. Francis Williams, Thomas Warnerton, and Ambrose Gibbons all continued in office in Portsmouth, as did Edward Hilton, Thomas Wiggin, and William Waldron in Dover.

Massachusetts–New Hampshire Laws

Massachusetts Bay had laws regulating most human behavior. The death penalty could be invoked upon conviction for any of a long list of crimes, including murder, idolatry, blasphemy, kidnapping, and treason. The death penalty was seldom inflicted, but the possible sentence acted as a deterrent to wrongdoing. Whipping, the pillory, and the stocks were the penalties for minor offenses such as working on the Sabbath or smoking in public. There was a scale of fines for various misdemeanors. If the criminal could not or would not pay, he was held up to public humiliation in the stocks. The Puritans understood the correctional value of social disapproval.

Drunkenness was punishable by a fine of five shillings or a whipping. A man could be fined or whipped if caught kissing a woman on the street. Swearing brought a fine or a whipping, though the incorrigibly profane risked having their tongues bored through with a hot iron. The seventeenth century was inured to pain and did not hesitate to use branding or maiming as punishment for those they considered hardened or particularly vicious offenders.

Dress was governed by a series of restrictions. Women might not bare their bosoms or their arms. They were forbidden to wear embroidery or needlework on their caps. No one, man or woman, was permitted to wear gold or silver belts, or hatbands. Men's coats might have one slit at the back and one at each cuff to allow a glimpse of the finery beneath, but no more. Ruffs and beaver hats were forbidden.

It is doubtful that the New Hampshire people paid much attention to any of these restrictions or that any attempt was made to enforce them. In workaday Portsmouth, Dover, Exeter, and Hampton there was not as yet the wealth that tempted Boston people to adorn themselves extravagantly.

No law was passed and no punishment set, but in 1648 the governor, deputy governor, and magistrates issued a proclamation that was meant to be heeded both in Massachusetts Bay and in New Hampshire.

> Forasmuch as the wearing of long hair after the manner of ruffians and barbarous Indians, has begun to invade New England, contrary to the rule of God's word, which says it is a shame for a man to wear long hair, we do declare and manifest our dislike and detestation against the wearing of such long hair, as against a thing uncivil and unmanly, whereby men do deform themselves and corrupt good manners.

The Quakers

The Quakers, or members of the Society of Friends, originated in England in the mid-seventeenth century. They were disciples of the religious mystic and social reformer George Fox, who preached the doctrine of the "inner light" and advocated a simplicity of life that extended to dress and speech. These Friends then were distinctly not, as they became, a quiet and gentle people. They were militant reformers who considered it their duty to overthrow accepted forms of religious belief and worship and to supplant them with their own.

The Quakers believed in separation of church and state. They refused to take oaths of allegience or to perform military service and did not acknowledge the clergy as superior or even different from anybody else. They did not believe in original sin, the resurrection of the body, or baptism. Zealously and fanatically the Quakers pushed their beliefs throughout Europe, then invaded America.

Massachusetts Bay was filled with horror at these agitators, who denied everything the Puritans held sacred. They wished fervently that the Friends would go away. Instead, to call attention to the rightness of their ways and the wrongness of all others, the Quakers desecrated the Puritan Sabbath. They burst into religious meetings with blackened faces and cried out against the minister and congregation in the Old South Meetinghouse itself. Two Quaker women, in a religious frenzy, ran naked through the Boston streets. In the eyes of the authorities of Massachusetts Bay the Quakers were "a cursed set of heretics lately risen up in the world," and they passed strict laws against them.

Laws Against Quakers

On October 14, 1658, Massachusetts banished Quakers from its jurisdiction, which included New Hampshire. If any were caught, they were to be "forwith committed to the house of correction, and at their entrance to be severely whipt, and kept constantly to work—and none suffered to converse or speak with them during their imprisonment." Any shipmaster caught bringing Quakers into Massachusetts Bay, New Hampshire, or Maine would be fined £100, imprisoned until the fine was paid, then made to take the Quakers back whence he had brought them. Anyone importing Quaker writings would be fined £5 for each piece of writing; anyone defending Quakers would be fined 40 shillings for a first offense, £4 for a second, jailed and then banished for further offense. Harboring a Quaker was made punishable by a fine of 40 shillings an hour.

Undeterred, the Quakers continued to come, and continued to harass other people. More severe laws were passed. These laws decreed that any male Quaker who returned after banishment would have one ear severed. If he returned again, he would lose the other ear. Quakers who returned a third time would have their tongues skewered with a hot iron. Those who persisted in returning after banishment would be put to death.

Even the intolerant Puritans had no wish to inflict such penalties. Strong-willed, iron-fisted Governor John Endecott himself pleaded with the Quakers not to return. Convinced of the righteousness of their mission and of God's inspiration and guidance, some Friends deliberately courted martyrdom, and won.

Quaker Hangings in Boston

Willliam Robinson, Marmaduke Stevenson, and Mary Dyer, who was the wife of the Secretary of Rhode Island, were banished in September 1659. All returned to Massachusetts. On October 27, 1659, they were escorted to a gallows on Boston Common by a hundred soldiers. The Reverend John Wilson railed at the condemned from the foot of the scaffold, and their voices were drowned by a continuous beating of drums. The two men were hanged and their bodies cast without ceremony into a pit. The rope was around Mrs. Dyer's neck when her son, who had sped from Rhode Island, got her reprieved on his promise to take her away. Despite the pleading of son and husband, Mrs. Dyer returned once more. Even then she was offered her freedom if she would promise to go away and stay away. She refused, saying, "In obedience to the will of the Lord I came, and in his will will I abide faithful unto death." She was hanged.

A Quaker named Wenlock Christison stormed into the courtroom in Boston's Town House, pointed his finger at the judges and shouted, "I am come here to warn ye that ye shed no more innocent blood!" He was dragged off to jail and three months later sentenced to death, but he was never executed. When Charles II came to the English throne in the Restoration of 1660, he ordered that the law condemning banished Quakers to death be repealed and that all Quakers still in prison be sent to London for trial.

Richard Waldron

Richard Waldron was born in England in 1616. A man of some estate, he bought property at Dover Neck in New Hampshire, returned to England, married, and came back to Dover about 1640. Waldron built a sawmill and went into the fur trade with the Indians. He built more sawmills, extended his fur trading, and somehow obtained large grants of land from Massachusetts Bay. Wealthy when he came, Waldron grew wealthier and more powerful. He was a perennial office holder. To protect his large interests, he got himself elected first a Dover selectman, then town treasurer, then a judge. In 1654, a strong proponent of Massachusetts rule in New Hampshire under which he had benefited so vastly, he was elected a deputy to the General Court in Boston. Elected year after year, he was seven times its speaker.

On December 22, 1662, sitting as a magistrate, Richard Waldron passed this sentence.

> To the Constables of Dover, Hampton, Salisbury, Newbury, Ipswich, Wenham, Lynn, Boston, Roxbury, Dedham, and until these vagabond Quakers are out of this jurisdiction.
>
> You and every of you are required in the King's Majesty's name, to take these vagabond Quakers, Anna Coleman, Mary Tompkins and Alice Ambrose and make them fast to the cart's tail; and draw the cart through your several towns, to whip them upon their naked backs, not exceeding ten stripes apiece on each of them, in each town; and so convey them from constable to constable till they are out of this jurisdic-

tion, as you will answer it at your peril; and this shall be your warrant. Per me, Richard Waldron.

The weather was cold. The suffering of the three women was severe. Many did not approve. One man did something about it.

Walter Barefoot

Dr. Walter Barefoot, one of the most colorful men in seventeenth-century New Hampshire, was then practicing medicine in Dover. Like Waldron, he was an influential and commanding figure but, unlike Waldron, he was of the New Hampshire faction that strongly opposed Massachusetts Bay.

In Salisbury, with the connivance of a magistrate, Barefoot took the tormented women away from the constable on the pretext that he would deliver them to the constable in Newbury. Instead, he set them free and helped them escape the jurisdiction of Massachusetts Bay. According to John N. McClintock in his *History of New Hampshire* (1888) the women fled to Rhode Island, the Barbados, or Nova Scotia—a wide choice.

Barefoot was a gadfly to the Massachusetts government. He banged about joyously, was arrested for swearing "horrid oaths," and was accused of bigamy and of deserting a wife in England (a favorite charge when colonists proved unsatisfactory to the colonial magistrates). In 1671, Barefoot was forbidden by Massachusetts Bay magistrate to practice medicine anywhere in Massachusetts or New Hampshire and was ordered to return to England by the next ship. Of course, he did not go, though no more is heard of his practicing medicine. Perhaps he was just too busy, for Barefoot became involved in many deals and disputes. Certainly he put an end to the one instance of legal barbarity in New Hampshire.

Witchcraft

Witches were even more devilish, literally, in colonial New England than Quakers. Belief in witches was general, among the educated as well as among the ignorant, in both Europe and America. Joan of Arc was burned at the stake as a witch in 1431. Scores of witches were put to death in Sweden. In England witches were executed under Cromwell just as they had been under Queen Elizabeth. Witchcraft was an established and frightening fact in the public consciousness. Some people were possessed of the Devil. They were evil spirits who wrought harm to the innocent in terrible ways. In every community there were gnarled and wrinkled old women who, people were convinced, could cast an evil eye on them, causing death or torment. Belief in witches by ministers, officials, and philosophers as well as the mass of the people was to culminate in Massachusetts Bay in the ghastly Salem witchcraft trials, which caused the arrest and imprisonment of 150 suspects, the hysterical confessions of fifty-five helpless men and women, and the execution of twenty-two innocent people.

New Hampshire Witches

New Hampshire got its first witchcraft scare in 1656. Toward evening of March 30 in that year, Susannah Trimmings of Portsmouth parted from Goodwife Barton at a freshet near the Barton house. On her way to her own home Mrs. Trimmings heard a rustling in the woods. She thought at first it was a pig, but a woman who seemed to be Goodwife Walford appeared, asked her where her husband was, and demanded to borrow a pound of cotton. When the loan was refused, she vanished in the form of a cat, and Goodwife Trimmings felt herself struck hard on the back by what seemed to be a clap of fire. She managed to make her way home but was ill for days.

Mrs. Trimmings testified to all this before three magistrates, on April 18, 1656. She said that Goodwife Walford "had on her head a white linen hood tied under her chin, and her waistcoat and petticoat were red, with an old green apron and a black hat on her head." Obviously this was the costume of a witch.

Oliver Trimmings supported his wife's testimony but was factual in his account and sensibly made no wild accusations. In describing his wife's condition, he deposed:

> She passed by me with her child in her arms, laid the child on the bed, sat down on the chest and leaned upon her elbow. Three times I asked her how she did.—She could not speak. I took her in my arms and held her up and repeated the question. She forced breath, and something stopped in her throat as if it would have stopped her breath. I unlaced her clothes and soon she spake and said, Lord have mercy upon me, this wicked woman will kill me. I asked her what woman. She said, Goodwife Walford. I tried to persuade her it was only weakness. She told me no, and related as above, that her back was as a flame of fire, and her lower parts were as it were numb and without feeling. I pinched her and she felt not. She continued very ill that night and the day and the night following very ill, and is still bad of her limbs and complains still daily about it.

Other witnesses had their complaints about Goodwife Walford. Nicholas Rowe averred that a woman had come to him one night when he was in bed and put her hand on his chest so that he could not speak and was in great pain until morning. The witch did not say anything to him, but Rowe thought from the light of a fire in the next room that it was Goodwife Waldron. Not only that, the next week she came and did it again.

Then came a witness for the defense, who testified that Goodwife Walford was at home "and as well as ever in her life" at the time Goodwife Trimmings claimed she was bewitched. Agnes Puddington demolished the alibi by swearing that a little after sunset one night she saw what she took to be a yellowish cat. Her husband got his gun to shoot it, but the cat leaped up into a tree, and the gun, bewitched, refused to fire.

On this assorted testimony Goodwife Walford was arrested on suspicion of being a witch. She was acquitted and instead of being hanged sued a certain Robert Church for slander for calling her a witch, won her case, and was awarded £5 damages and court costs. It was much safer to be called a witch in tolerant New Hampshire than in credulous Massachusetts Bay.

Nevertheless, Eunice Cole was convicted of witchcraft in 1656, whipped, and sent to jail in Boston under a life sentence. After ten or twelve years she was returned to Hampton, where the town maintained her as a pauper. Then, about 1672, someone who did not like her acccused Mary Greenland, wife of Dr. Henry Greenland, a friend of Walter Barefoot, of the same thing. No prosecution ensued, and that was the end of the witchcraft scare in New Hampshire. No one there seemed to take it too seriously. People had more to fear from another quarter.

The Mason Claims

The Mason family could do nothing to press their claims to New Hampshire under Cromwell, for they were Royalists. After the Restoration and the coming of age of Robert Tufton, who under the terms of his grandfather's will took the Mason surname, the family looked to the court of Charles II for help, and got it. Their claims were valid under crown grants and were recognized as just. Joseph Mason, a kinsman, was sent to New England as the agent of Mrs. Anne Mason, and he began trying to reassert the ownership of what was legally part of the Mason inheritance. He met with little success.

People in Portsmouth held land, houses, and other property on which Captain John Mason had expended a fortune. They claimed the houses and other property by right of possession, as recompense for services rendered, and maintained that the land had been awarded to them by town grants from what had been Strawbery Banke. They appealed to Massachusetts Bay for protection against the Mason claims.

They had another weapon. Captain Bryan Pendleton had transferred himself and his considerable possessions to Portsmouth from Watertown, Massachusetts. He became chairman of the Portsmouth selectmen on April 5, 1652. That same night he and the other selectmen destroyed or concealed those parts of the town records that lent validity to the Mason claims. Possession being proverbially nine points of the law and with this safeguard thoughtfully provided by Pendleton, the Portsmouth people who had simply taken what Mason owned continued to hold it with a greater sense of security. For his enterprise, Captain Pendleton was sent as Portsmouth's deputy to the General Court, a post he held for ten years.

Joseph Mason returned to England, leaving Nicholas Shapleigh as attorney for the Mason interests. Shapleigh began to lease land in New Hampshire to his friends, among them Walter Barefoot. Major Robert Pike, a leader in Salisbury and popular in Dover, also recognized the justice of the Mason claims, as did other important men, but people like the Cutt, Pendleton, Fryar, Waldron, and Stileman families, who held some of the best land in Portsmouth, including valuable shore property, refused to acknowledge any debt to Mason. When Barefoot and Edward Hilton of Exeter took tracts of land on the Lamperell River, they reserved a yearly rental for the lord proprietor, but others did not follow their example. About a thousand families, Robert Tufton Mason claimed, were squatting on his New Hampshire land.

Accusations, recriminations, and involved litigation continued for many years. In a number of major instances the dispute was between wealthy Puritans like Waldron, who intended to keep everything they had obtained through Massachusetts grants, and Church of England Loyalists like Barefoot.

Boston, of course, backed its own. Massachusetts Bay claimed New Hampshire for herself, thus did not recognize the grants which the Council for New England had made to Captain John Mason, or the manor he had bequeathed to his grandchildren, any more than it recognized the Gorges' ownership of Maine. When justice interfered with practicality, or piety with possible gain, Massachusetts Bay seldom nad any difficulty in making its choice.

The King's Commission

After the Restoration, in a move to reassert royal authority, King Charles II dispatched a commission to report on conditions in England's American possessions. Sir Robert Carr, Samuel Maverick, Colonel Richard Nichols, and George Cartwright were all members of the commission. They were courteously received in the Middle Atlantic and southern colonies, but were treated with scant civility in Massachusetts Bay.

In its report, the commission charged that Massachusetts arrogantly acted as a free state and had once petitioned Cromwell to be so declared. The report claimed that under its original charter Massachusetts had the power to make and execute its own laws "and that they are not obliged to the King, but by civility." The commissioners noted that Massachusetts Bay did not permit its people the freedom granted Englishmen at home. It admitted none but its church members to the franchise and persecuted all religious groups except the Congregational. It had executed Quakers and "They have beaten some to jelly, and been . . . exceeding cruell to others."

The report went on to say that the Massachusetts Bay authorities fined any who observed Christmas Day £5; they exacted whatever taxes they chose, but would give no accounting of moneys collected. "They convert Indians by hiring them to come and hear sermons . . . which the more generous natives scorn."

Massachusetts, the commission reported, claimed lands belonging to Rhode Island, Plymouth, and Connecticut as well as Fort Albany in New York and, from that point, all the land to the South Seas, although its agents had made their maps by guess. ". . . on the east they have usurped Captain Mason's and Sir Ferdinando's patents."

Condition of Portsmouth

The commissioners collided head on with Massachusetts when Carr, Cartwright, and Maverick arrived in Portsmouth in July 1665. On the Piscataqua River they found "an excellent harbor, large and safe and seven or eight ships in it, and a great store of masts." They ordered the four New Hampshire towns to fortify the harbor. Thereupon Massachusetts Bay immediately dispatched two marshals to the four towns with warrants countermanding the order.

Such actions provoked the New Hampshire people, but when a Portsmouth tavern keeper, Abraham Corbet, dared circulate a petition to the King asking for a government for New Hampshire separate from that of

Massachusetts Bay, he was seized and jailed in Boston. Sir Robert Carr went there and attempted to post bail for Corbet, but none was allowed. While Sir Robert was in Boston, another man complained of injustice in the Massachusetts courts, and for this impudence he was promptly fined £50. The next year Abraham Corbet was fined £20 and £5 costs, and forbidden to retail liquor or ever hold town office in New Hampshire. It was just not tactful to oppose rich and tyrannical Massachusetts Bay.

Charles II recalled his commission in 1666 and, partly as a result of its report, ordered Massachusetts Bay to send a delegation to England to defend itself before the Lords of Trade and Plantations and to show cause why its charter should not be revoked.

Portsmouth was now the most prosperous of the New Hampshire towns. Its merchants were accumulating wealth, some of them great wealth. In one of his petitions to the crown, Robert Tufton Mason wrote in 1671:

> New Hampshire is a place the best improved for land and most populated of any in these parts; abounding plentifully with corn, cattle, timber and fish; and the people live generally very comfortably and happy; having a good trade to all parts, and stores of shipping at their town. Portsmouth, which exports and imports yearly some thousands of tons of goods, of their own growth and foreign. Goods exported yearly are 20,000 tons of deals [pine boards] and pipestaves, 10,000 quintals of fish, ten shiploads of masts, and several thousand of beaver and otter skins. The imports are 300 tons of wine and brandy, 200 tons of goods from the Leeward Islands, and 200 tons of salt.

Mason may have exaggerated a little. Certainly Boston and its environs were more populous and prosperous, but there is little reason to question his supporting statistics.

CHAPTER FOUR

The Royal Province of New Hampshire

In 1677, after trying for years to get it for nothing, Massachusetts Bay bought Maine from Ferdinando Gorges, grandson of the original lord proprietor, for £1,250, thus obtaining a considerable piece of real estate for a small sum. It was unable to retain New Hampshire at any price.

In 1679 New Hampshire was declared a royal province, directly subject to the crown. This change was made in England, not for the benefit of the people on the Piscataqua, but in order to strip insolent Massachusetts Bay of some of her pretensions and to clear the way for the Mason heirs to prosecute their claims.

President John Cutt

As a royal province, New Hampshire had a president and council appointed by the crown and an assembly elected by the freemen of the province. Its first president was John Cutt. Born in Wales, his father a member of Cromwell's Parliament, John Cutt had come to New Hampshire with his brothers, Robert and Richard, in 1646. Richard Cutt settled on one of the Isles of Shoals, where he carried on a fishery. Later, captain of a military company, he moved to Great Island, then to a great house in Portsmouth. Ultimately he was the wealthiest man in New Hampshire.

John Cutt became a merchant and, like his brother, very rich. These "merchants" were not shopkeepers, selling notions and penny candy. They were importers and exporters on a large scale, buyers and sellers of cargoes of lumber, furs, fish, wine, sugar, and other commodities, which they often shipped in their own vessels. They were businessmen, traders in international commerce.

President Cutt had a large estate, obtained through grants from Massachusetts Bay, which he knew would be invalid if Robert Mason's claims were allowed. Some of the members of his council were in a similar fix. They took office largely to protect their property and to keep others out of office who might dispute their claims to lands. They were politicians who, like politicians at any time, seek public office for private gain and are in conflict with other politicians with the same end in view.

In point of wealth and useful family connections, the Cutt, Vaughan, and Waldron families were among the first in the new province. They owned virtually all of "the Banke," and they intended to keep it that way. One of John Cutt's daughters married Richard Waldron, Jr., and another married wealthy merchant Samuel Penhallow, who became a successful politician, chief justice of the province, and eventually historian of New Hampshire's Indian wars.

Provincial Laws

As a royal province, New Hampshire was subject to the laws of England, but it also drew up its own code of laws.

Idolatry, blasphemy, murder, treason, bearing false witness, witchcraft, and a variety of abnormal sexual practices were all capital crimes, punishable by death. Any kind of murder, whether premeditated and willful or unplanned, and even manslaughter brought the death penalty on conviction—which was hard to obtain. Cursing or striking a parent, rape, and arson were also capital crimes. What is now called kidnapping was then "manstealing," and the prescribed penalty read "If any man stealeth mankind, he shall be put to death or otherwise grievously punished." The penalty for another crime was this:

> If any man have a rebellious or stubborn son of sufficient years and understanding, viz. 16 years of age or upwards wch shall not obey ye voyce of his father or ye voyce of his mother, yt when they have chastened him will not hearken unto them, then shall his father and mother, being his naturall

> parents, bring him before the Magistrates assembled in court, and testifie unto them that their son is rebellious and stubborne, and will not obey their voyce and chastizes but lives in sundry notorious crimes, such son shall be put to death or otherwise severely punished.

Adultery was punished by several whippings, and those convicted had to wear the capital letters "AD" cut in cloth and sewed on the sleeves or back of their uppermost garments. If at any time they were found without these identifying letters, they were publicly whipped.

Burglary by housebreaking or robbing a person was rewarded the first time by having the letter "B" branded on the right hand. On a second offense, the convicted thief would be branded also on the left hand and severely whipped. If the burglary was committed on the Sabbath, the brand was burned into the criminal's forehead—". . . and if he shall fall into the like offence the 3rd time he shall be put to death as incorageable, or otherwise severely punished as ye court shall determine."

As in the other northern English possessions in America, drunkenness was widely prevalent in New Hampshire. The province defined it clearly. "By drunkenness is to be understood one yt lisps or falters in his speech by reason of over much drink, or yet staggers in his going or y'vomitts by reason of excessive drinking, or that cannot by reason thereof follow his calling." Drunks were either fined or locked in the stocks. A fourth offense could be punished by public whipping. Swearing, too, was punishable by fines or commitment to the stocks.

Severe penalties were meted out for bribery, forgery, defacing records, burning or tearing down fences, and gambling. There was another offense that New Hampshire would not countenance.

> It is therefore ordered and enacted by this General Assembly, That w'pson soever in this Government shall pfane ye Lord's Day by doeing unnecessary worke or travell, or by sports or recreation, or by dining at ordinarys in time of publique worship, such pson or psons shall forfeit 10s, or be whipt for every such offence, and if it appears ye sin was proudly or presumptuously, and with a high hand committed

against ye known command and authority of ye Blessed God, such person therein dispising and reproaching ye Lord, shall be sevearly punished at ye Judmt of ye Court.

Any member of the Council was empowered to marry people, provided the couple had announced their intentions three times at some public meeting or posted them on the meetinghouse door in public view. Innkeepers were forbidden to sell liquor to children or servants. Such were some of the laws and the penalties for their transgression adopted by the province of New Hampshire. There was also a basic privilege.

The Right to Vote

The franchise was not universal. As elsewhere, property qualifications were required as a sign of responsibility. Nor was the vote given those considered immature. There was also a religious qualification.

> It is ordered by this Assembly and the authority thereof, yt all Englishmen, being Protestants, yt are settled Inhabitants and freeholders in any towne of this Province, of ye age of 24 years, not viceous in life but of honest and good conversation, and such as have 24 *l* Rateable Estate wth out heads of persons having also taken the oath of allegiance to his Maj, and no others, shall be admitted to ye liberty of being freemen of this Province, and to give their vote for the choice of Deputies to the Generall Assembly, Constables, Selectmen, Jurors and other officers and concernes in ye townes where they dwell; provided this order gives no liberty to any pson to vote in the dispossion or distribution of any lands, timber or other properties in ye towne, but such as have reall right thereto; and if any difference arise about sd right of voting, it shall be judged and determined by ye Presidt and Council with the Genll Assembly of this Province.

Lieutenant Governor Edward Cranfield

President John Cutt died in 1681. He was succeeded briefly by Richard Waldron, who was already commander of the New Hampshire militia, which consisted of a company of infantry in each town, one troop of cavalry, and one company of artillery at the fort. Cutt's and Waldron's were but stopgap appointments at best. These New Hampshire men presided only until Edward Cranfield arrived in Portsmouth in October 1682, and published his King's commission as lieutenant governor and commander in chief of the royal province of New Hampshire.

Cranfield's commission gave him great powers, and he promptly extended them so as to give himself almost arbitrary rule of the province. Robert Tufton Mason, styled proprietor, was immediately made one of Cranfield's council. Of the old council, Richard Waldron, William Vaughan, and several others were retained. Walter Barefoot and Richard Chamberlain were added. A week after his arrival Cranfield suspended Waldron.

A hanger-on at the English court, Cranfield had come from an impoverished if prominent family. He received his commission through Mason influence—an influence that was probably exerted by Edward Randolph, a Mason kinsman who had been active at court in getting New Hampshire separated from Massachusetts Bay. Cranfield had acquired a share in the Mason interests. He was out to recoup his fortunes and did not care how he did it.

As lieutenant governor, Cranfield organized the courts to favor the claims of Mason against the people living on what he held to be his lands. Inevitably these courts found for the claimant, dispatching many cases in a single day but charging exorbitant costs for each one. Robert Mason obtained the judgments he sought, but he was unable to act upon them. When the estates of those against whom decisions were made were put up for sale, no purchasers could be found for them. Thus the New Hampshire people retained possession of what they had held for almost fifty years, land they had worked and had often defended against the Indians.

Needing money, Cranfield forced the General Assembly to pass an act for raising funds through taxation. The constables of the various towns either forgot or refused to collect these taxes, so a special agent

 was appointed. When he came to Hampton, he was beaten and his sword snatched from him. A rope was tied around his neck, and his feet were fastened together beneath the belly of his horse. So mounted and bedecked, he was driven from the province.

When the provost marshal for New Hampshire tried to collect taxes at the home of a man in Portsmouth, the wife of a certain William Cotton called him a rogue who consorted only with rogues and rascals, and threatened to scald him with hot water. A marshal sent to Exeter fared no better. The leading women of the town assured him that they had a red-hot spit and plenty of scalding water ready for his reception. He returned empty-handed to Portsmouth.

Determined to exert the absolute power he had assumed, Cranfield dissolved the assembly. This move of the vindictive lieutenant governor served only to increase the resentment and hatred of the people.

Edward Gove

In one famous instance Cranfield's misrule provoked outright mutiny. Although he was unable to persuade other men to join him, Edward Gove of Hampton armed himself, his son, and a servant and, on January 27, 1683, started for Exeter, seven miles to the north, to stand up for his rights. A justice of the peace tried to stop him, but Gove pushed on and was joined by eight more protesters before they were arrested by foot soldiers.

Gove declared that Edward Cranfield's commission was invalid because it had been signed in Scotland. He accused the lieutenant governor of trying to bring popery into New Hampshire and swore that his sword was drawn against him.

Gove's was a demonstration of dissent, but its consequences were serious for him. On February 1, 1683, he was indicted for treason by a grand jury. He was tried and condemned. Judge Richard Waldron pronounced the dread sentence:

> You shall be carried back to the place whence you came, and from thence be drawn to the place of execution, and there be hanged by the neck, and cut down alive; your entrails shall

> be taken out and burned before your face, your head cut off, and your body divided into four quarters; and your head and quarters be disposed of at the king's pleasure.

This was the standard penalty for treason in the seventeenth century. Governments at that time did not encourage dissent.

Cranfield was all for exacting the punishment at once, saying fearfully that he would not feel safe until it was carried out. Since the prison was out of repair, Gove was given in charge of Captain Walter Barefoot at New Castle. He was kept in irons, which were five feet seven inches long, two men locked together, and kept in durance vile under, as he wrote, "a good keeper, a hard captain."

Petitions to save him were circulated immediately. They succeeded. On June 6, 1683, Gove was delivered to the Tower of London, where he was kept for two years at a cost of £3 per week. He was pardoned in 1685 after his wife's plea that he was both drunk and suffering from a streak of inherited insanity at the time of his misdeed. Gove himself said strangely that if he had known that what he was doing was against the law, he would not have done it. He was returned to New Hampshire, King James II ordering that all his property and possessions be restored to him just as if he had never been convicted. Gove was unwell after his triumphant return. He claimed that he had been fed poison in prison.

The Reverend Joshua Moody

Cranfield took less serious moves against Gove with the same bitterness, and his treatment of those he suspected was harsh. Richard Waldron himself was several times arrested for "mutinous and seditious Words." Then Joshua Moody, pastor of the Puritan church in Portsmouth, fell victim to Cranfield.

The collector of the port one day seized a ketch for violation of some of the many laws of trade. During the night a group of men repossessed the vessel and took her out of the harbor. When tried for complicity in the crime, the owner of the ship, a member of Moody's congregation, protested his innocence, and the charges were dropped. A local historian hints that bribery may have helped get the shipowner exonerated, for he says that Cranfield "forgave him all."

This acquittal did not satisfy the conscience of the Reverend Joshua Moody. He applied to Cranfield for evidence to present before his church. Cranfield refused, so Moody preached a sermon against false swearing, and the erring shipowner confessed. Thus Moody proved that the civil judgment had been wrong.

Cranfield was incensed. Immediately he dispatched a sheriff with a notice to Moody that he and some of his friends wished to partake of Communion the following Sunday. He ordered Moody to administer it according to the rites of the Church of England. Moody refused. Haled into court, he protested that he was not an ordained clergyman of the Anglican church so was not authorized to administer the sacrament in that way. He also pointed out that the statute of uniformity was not in force in New England.

Four of the six judges voted for Moody's acquittal but, hectored by Cranfield, three changed their minds, finally only two dissented. The Reverend Joshua Moody was found guilty, and Cranfield promptly issued this order for his arrest:

> New-Hampshire in New England
>
> To James Sherlock, gent. prov. marshall and sheriff of the said province or his deputy
>
> In his majesty's name you are hereby required forthwith to take and apprehend the body and person of Joshua Moody of Portsmouth in the said province, and carry him to the prison of great Island in the said province; and the prisonkeeper, Richard Abbot, is hereby required to receive him the said Joshua Moody and keep him in safe custody in the same prison, he having been *convicted of administring the sacraments contrary to the laws and statutes of England, and refusing to administer the sacraments according to the rites and ceremonies of the church of England, and the form enjoined in*

the said statutes. There to remain for the space of six months next ensuing without bail or mainprize.

Dat. the 6th of Feb. 1683/4

Walt. Barefoot
Peter Coffin
Hen. Green
Hen. Roby

With Moody in prison was another important man of Portsmouth, William Vaughan. Married to a daughter of President Cutt, Vaughan was a wealthy merchant who had been in the council under his father-in-law and even for a time under Cranfield. He was a major in the militia, had been a judge at Gove's trial, and would eventually become chief justice of New Hampshire's Superior Court.

Vaughan had been jailed without conviction of any crime. Cranfield merely wanted to get one of the most adverse critics of his administration out of the way. The order for his arrest accused him of "having refused to find security for his said good behavior." Why should he? Vaughan asked. He had done nothing.

Vaughan feared the worse, and he proved to be an accurate prophet. "I am credibly informed, and you may believe it," he wrote, "that the governor did in the open council yesterday, say and swear dreadfully, that he would put the province into the greatest confusion and distraction he could possibly, and then go away and leave them so, and the devil take them. He also said that Mr. Mason said he would drive them into a second rebellion, but himself would do it before. . . ."

Vaughan was imprisoned for many months, but Moody was released after thirteen weeks, during which his church had been closed. Forbidden to preach again in New Hampshire, he went to Boston as assistant pastor of its First Church. By advice of a council of ministers, without which he would not venture, he returned and resumed his Portsmouth pulpit in 1693, but before he left Boston he spoke his mind once again and showed the courage of his convictions.

 A man and his wife, charged with witchcraft, were in jail but allowed to go free during the day. The day before they were to be sent to Salem for trial, Moody invited them to worship, and he preached from the text, "When they persecute you in this city, flee ye into another" (Matthew 10:23). After the service he called on the accused in prison and advised them to escape. He sent them to New York, whose governor received them at his own house. They stayed in New York a year, then returned to Salem after the witchcraft frenzy had subsided.

Joshua Moody died in 1697.

Mason and Barefoot versus Wiggin and Nutter

One dispute arising from the Mason claims did not reach the court. Robert Mason was staying in the home of Walter Barefoot, one of his chief supporters. In December 1685, Barefoot's brother-in-law, Thomas Wiggin of Dover, and his friend, big, rough, strong-willed Anthony Nutter, who was a millowner and the largest taxpayer on Bloody Point, paid Mason and Barefoot a formal call.

During the visit Wiggin became so abusive in denouncing Mason's claims that Mason took him by the arm and urged him to the door, saying he would not be insulted in his own house. Thus encouraged, Wiggin grasped Mason by his cravat, yanked him to the chimney, threw him into the fire, and began to strangle him. When Barefoot tried to drag his brother-in-law off Mason, Wiggin and Nutter threw him into the fire too. While Mason was screaming for a servant to bring him his sword, Walter Barefoot somehow lost one tooth and won two broken ribs.

Dismissal of Cranfield

Conditions in New Hampshire had become insupportable. Its people sent a representative to England with a long list of complaints against Edward Cranfield. In effect, they said that Cranfield had ignored the provincial assembly and ruled arbitrarily, that he had by purchase of mortgages from Robert Mason made himself owner of the province and was not likely to act impartially, that he had appointed judges who favored the Mason claims, that court costs were excessive though nothing was accomplished, that men were made to post large bonds for unspecified crimes, that ministers were denied religious freedom, that the only laws made were those enacted by the lieutenant governor in council or laws he had directed the General Assembly to make. There were other charges, among them that Cranfield refused to accept lumber and staves at specified rates in lieu of cash, which was customary in New Hampshire.

As a result, Edward Cranfield was censured by the crown and soon removed from office. He left New England for the West Indies. In time he was made collector of the port of Barbados and became a changed man. He made it a point to be markedly courteous to shipmasters from Portsmouth and to any other travelers from New Hampshire.

Walter Barefoot, ribs healed but still missing a tooth, succeeded Cranfield. He ruled as lieutenant governor of New Hampshire for just one year.

CHAPTER FIVE

Indian Wars

Passaconaway, great chief and medicine man of the Pennacooks in New Hampshire, counseled peace and friendship with the English, and until he relinquished authority to his son Numphow in 1660, his counsels were heeded. Peace prevailed, and the Indians frequented the towns along the Piscataqua and traded amicably with the colonists.

Slaughter of the Pequots

Massachusetts Bay, Plymouth, and Connecticut were early at war with the Indians. Conveniently the Puritans saw them as devils spawned of Satan who, the orthodox believed, had ruled North America until their coming. They tried to subject them to English law, which the Indians did not understand. They cheated them out of their lands, destroyed their hunting grounds, and punished any offense, real or fancied, with barbarous reprisals.

As early as 1636, after the Indians had murdered a dissolute trader, John Endecott and a hundred men laid waste a whole Indian village on Block Island. The next year John Underhill of Massachusetts Bay, with a small force and some Mohican allies, joined a John Mason (*not* New Hampshire's Captain John Mason) leading ninety Connecticut men and several hundred Narragansett and Niantic allies, and together they surrounded a Pequot fort near what is now Stonington, Connecticut. They set fire to the enclosure, which held four or five hundred Indian men, women, and children, burning many of them alive, and methodically shot or tomahawked those who tried to escape. Mason and Underhill were hailed as heroes, and the victorious Massachusetts and Plymouth colonists raised the severed heads and hands of slain Indians on poles to enrage the foe.

The Hundred Years' War

Naturally these unpleasant facts were known to the New Hampshire Indians, but since they were enemies to some of the tribes involved, they remained generally quiet for a long time. The first of five Indian wars was a concerted revolt by the Indians against treatment by Massachusetts Bay and Plymouth; the others were the four wars between England and France, in which the Indians fought with the French. The five wars were:

King Philip's War	1675–1676
King William's War	1689–1697
Queen Anne's War	1701–1713
King George's War	1740–1748
French and Indian War	1754–1763

It can be seen that, with short interruptions, these wars continued for about a hundred years but, as Clark Wissler points out in *Indians of the United States*, it is not inaccurate to say that, in New England, one long war began with the first English settlements and continued until about 1770.

King Philip's War

The Plymouth colonists had treated the Indians with great severity. Massachusetts Bay, with some settlements on the coast and more on the Connecticut River about a hundred miles to the west, had forcibly compressed the Indians into the unsettled region in between. The Indians saw the game on which they depended for food being killed off and their lands seized, sometimes under spurious agreements or certainly one-sided arrangements. Their tribal way of life was in danger of being wiped out.

The chief of the Wampanoags, King Philip, was peremptorily haled into Taunton and made to confess that he had broken treaties and covenants. Later in the year he was arrested, taken to Plymouth, and made to pay £40 for the expenses of the expedition sent to arrest him. Then the Wampanoags were forced to surrender all their firearms, and Philip was made to acknowledge his subjection to Plymouth as well as to England. When he tried to recover the confiscated guns of his people, he found that the sons and grandsons of the Pilgrim Fathers had simply distributed them among themselves.

Plotting revenge for the indignities to which he had been subjected and for the wrongs his people had suffered, King Philip called in the Nipmucks and the Narragansetts to join his Wampanoags. He also tried to enlist the Mohicans, but they refused.

A savage war ensued. Massachusetts and Plymouth were out to exterminate the Indians; the Indians were equally determined to exterminate the colonists. No quarter was given in a conflict marked by atrocities on both sides. The Indians raided and burned the outlying towns, massacring or carrying off their inhabitants. Taunton, Middleborough, Brookfield, Deerfield, Northampton, Springfield, Groton, Medfield, and many other towns suffered. Sixteen houses were destroyed in Plymouth itself. Thousands of braves and militiamen were involved in bloody fights, and many were killed.

The war came to an ugly end on Sunday, December 16, 1676, when a thousand colonists under Governor Josiah Winslow of Plymouth attacked the Narragansett stronghold at Mount Hope, Rhode Island. About two thousand Indians were inside the palisaded enclosure. They fought the attackers desperately, but though many of the colonists were killed, they fired the stronghold. About half the Indians perished in the flames as the Puritans filled the Sabbath afternoon with slaughter.

Betrayed by an Indian whose brother he had tomahawked, King Philip was hunted down in a swamp by soldiers under Captain Benjamin Church of Plymouth and shot through the heart. His body was quartered and hung in the trees. His head was shipped to Plymouth and displayed on a pole in the village common where people could see it as they went to the meetinghouse for a special service of thanksgiving.

More than six hundred men of Massachusetts Bay and Plymouth had been killed. Forty towns were severely damaged. Property loss was estimated at half a million pounds, but the Indians had been permanently subdued in southern New England. More than two thousand of them were killed in King Philip's War.

The happy conquerors executed many sachems and warriors as war criminals, scattered Indian women and children throughout the colonies as slaves, and by decree of the General Court shipped all adult male Indian captives into slavery outside New England. Many of them were sold in the West Indies, but as some planters considered the warriors useless as field hands, the Puritans could not find buyers for all of them. These people they simply abandoned on foreign shores. Although important Boston clergymen had advised that King Philip's son be killed, the boy and his mother were among those enslaved.

The Dover Treachery

New Hampshire was comparatively untouched by King Philip's War. Its fur trade with the Indians in the north, mostly Pennacooks and Abnakis, flourished. But New Hampshire was deeply involved in an aftermath of the war.

Some of the Indians who had fought under King Philip fled north and took refuge with the friendly Pennacooks on the upper Merrimack and with the Indians around Chocorua who, under a treaty made with Major Richard Waldron, were at peace with the English.

Waldron invited about four hundred Indians to a meeting near his home in Dover in early September, 1676. The Indians who had been dealing with Waldron for years and trusted him as a trader, friend, and "father," came willingly. The "strange" Indians came with the Pennacooks.

Captain William Hathorne, ancestor of Nathaniel Hawthorne, and two other Massachusetts Bay captains, Frost and Still, marched on Dover with a strong force and suggested to Waldron that they attack and wipe out the massed Indians. Waldron had a better idea. He proposed to the Indians that they engage in a mock battle with the English the next day. The Indians were delighted. When the war games began,

Waldron and the Massachusetts force allowed the Indians to fire first, wasting their shot. They then captured all of them without having to fire a single shot themselves.

The Pennacooks were allowed to go free. All of the strange Indians —about two hundred according to historian Belknap, three hundred by other accounts—were carried off to Boston. Seven or eight who were known to have killed colonists were executed. All of the others were sold into slavery. This was treachery which the strange Indians and the hitherto peaceful Pennacooks never forgot or forgave.

New Hampshire the Battleground

If New Hampshire escaped lightly in King Philip's War, it suffered more than southern New England in the wars that were about to begin. These were the declared wars in which England and France fought for possession of disputed territory. This time the Indians were caught between opposing European nations and their ambitions, and were forced to choose sides. Naturally they chose the side that treated them better, the one that promised and paid rewards and did not treat them as savages to be obliterated but as trusted allies.

The French were far wiser than the English in their relations with the Abnaki. They did not attempt to interfere with the Indian way of life or to make the Indians responsible to French law. They provided them with guns and ammunition. They paid them well for English scalps and for English captives sold in Canada as slaves. They sent skilled men to deal with the Indians and educated the understanding priests to convert them to Roman Catholicism, whose rituals and mysteries the Indians learned to value and cherish. Like the French, the Indians saw the English as heretics, so in part the Indian wars on New Hampshire were holy wars—which the Indians carried out in most unholy fashion.

This time the Indians and the colonists did not meet head on in pitched battles. Led by French officers or on their own, using the kind of guerrilla tactics at which they excelled, the Indians waged a baffling and deadly war. There were few noble savages among them, just as there were few bona fide saints among the settlers.

Skulking Indians spied out frontier towns and outlying farms. They lay in ambush, then sprang their traps. Men were slain as they worked in the fields and woods. The houses of unsuspecting inhabitants were suddenly in flames as the Indians hit and ran. Women and children were killed or bundled off on long and terrible flights to Canada. They were the slaves of their Indian captors until, if they survived the torture and torment of the trail, they became slaves of the French. Many did not survive. The weak or aged were promptly dispatched. The Indians smashed the heads of sick or complaining babies against trees before the eyes of their mothers. Young braves tortured captives just for the fun of it while their elders turned captives they disliked over to the squaws for more refined torture. Many of the tales recorded are ghastly and revolting.

Jeremy Belknap's Comment

Jeremy Belknap lists many instances of murder, looting, burning, and scalping, but even in 1784, when he published the first volume of his *History of New Hampshire*, he was fair. The Indians had been cheated by men who took their lands and defrauded them in trade. They were cruel and used fiendish tortures. They were revengeful. But so were the English, who exacted an eye for an eye and a tooth for a tooth. Indian jealousies and hatred, Belknap pointed out, were the same as those of their New Hampshire neighbors.

> Our historians have generally represented the Indians in a most odious light, especially when recounting the effects of their ferocity. Dogs, caitiffs, miscreants, and hell-hounds, are the politest names which have been given them by some writers, who seem to be in a passion at the mentioning of their cruelties, and at other times speak of them with contempt. . . .
>
> The *treachery* with which these people are justly charged, is exactly the same disposition which operates in the breach of solemn treaties between nations which call themselves christian. Can it be more criminal in an Indian, than in an European, not to think himself bound by promises and oaths extorted from him under duress?

Jeremy Belknap, a Congregational clergyman born in Boston, wrote the three-volume *History of New Hampshire* (1784, 1791, 1792).

The Indians never forgot an injury. They tortured those who had wronged them. At the same time, they never forgot a kindness, and there were many instances in which they repaid kindnesses shown to them or their ancestors. They sometimes carried captive children in their arms or on their shoulders, gave prisoners the best of the food when they had little themselves, and used herbs and simple remedies to care for captives who were ill. They never assaulted women. Not one instance of an Indian's sexually assaulting a white woman has been recorded.

Belknap could see both sides, but it was hard for New Hampshire people whose husbands or wives had been killed and scalped, whose homes had been destroyed, and whose children had been massacred or abducted to be dispassionate. For them it was "kill or be killed." People were forced to leave their homes and, for protection, to crowd into the largest and strongest houses, which were fortified by timber walls. Day and night, guards were on duty in sentry boxes on the roofs. Towns built garrisons around some buildings. There were constant alarms, and few of them were false.

The Indians visited exquisite tortures on prisoners they singled out for revenge. Men were buried to their faces and slowly suffocated. Some were dismembered, the Indians cutting off a finger or a toe each day until the victim died. William Moody was one of five men taken in a raid on Exeter. The Indians roasted him alive and, according to one writer, ate him. Two children were killed in a raid on Dover during Queen Anne's War. Since they did not have time to scalp them, the Indians cut off their heads and took them with them. Their scalps were worth money in Montreal.

The Dover Raid

Major Richard Waldron, who had sentenced the Quaker women and later Edward Gove, was made commander in chief of the New Hampshire military force on April 23, 1689. Late in June that same year his house was one of five in Dover which were garrisoned. People from neighboring houses slept there at night behind high timber walls with bolted doors.

One night a squaw hinted that trouble was coming, but either her words were not understood or they were disregarded. A young man told Waldron that the town was full of Indians and that people were greatly concerned. Waldron said that he had dealt with Indians all his life. Jestingly he told people to go plant their pumpkins; he would tell them when the Indians would break out.

The Indians that Waldron had sold into slavery had waited almost thirteen years for revenge. Some of them had escaped and returned. Planning carefully, they sent two Indian women to each garrison in Dover to ask leave to spend the night of June 27 by the fire. All but one garrison agreed, the people even showing the squaws how to unlock the garrison doors if they wished to go out at night. The squaws told Waldron that a number of Indians were coming the next day to trade, and one Indian, Mesandowit, asked, "Brother Waldron, what would you do if the strange Indians should come?" Waldron told him that he could assemble a hundred men just by lifting his finger.

After Waldron's garrison had retired, unaccountably leaving no guard, the squaws inside opened the door, and the warriors rushed in. Waldron drove back some with his sword, but one struck him from behind with his hatchet. The Indians forced the terrified inhabitants to bring them food. Then, after they had eaten and drunk, they placed Waldron in the chair from which he usually passed sentence.

"Who shall judge the Indians now?" they taunted.

Each of the attackers slashed him across the breast with his knife, saying, "I cross out my account."

The Indians then hacked off Waldron's nose and ears and stuffed them into his mouth. As he toppled from his chair, one of them placed Waldron's own sword so that he fell dead upon it.

The Indians raided all five garrisons at the same time. They killed fourteen (or fifty) and scalped them all, plus one more whom they took to be dead but who recovered. They plundered the houses, then fired them, and escaped with their prisoners. The militia gave chase and recaptured the prisoners but, their vengeance sated, the Indians escaped.

On this Dover raid William Wentworth, founder of the Wentworth dynasty in New Hampshire, was sleeping in Heard's garrison. Awakened by the barking of dogs just as the Indians attacked, Wentworth, who was about eighty years old, fell on his back and set his feet against the gate, holding off the Indians until his cries alarmed the people in the garrison. Two shots fired through the gate missed him. This first New Hampshire Wentworth lived to be over ninety years of age.

Hannah Dustin

In 1694 Ursula Cutt, the second wife and widow of President Cutt, and three men haying for her on the pretentious Cutt farm two miles above Portsmouth were killed and scalped. In July of the same year 250 Indians under a French officer named Villiers attacked settlements on the Oyster River. They were repulsed at some garrisons, but at others they killed or captured a hundred people and burned twenty houses. The Maine town of York had been destroyed by Indians in 1692. Four fortified houses managed to hold out, but the Indians killed about fifty people and carried off a hundred. York's minister was shot dead as he was mounting his horse at the door, and his wife and children were stolen.

Hannah Dustin and her baby were captured in Haverhill, Massachusetts, in 1697. On the way to Canada the Indians camped with their captives on a small island in the Merrimack near Penacook (which became first Rumford and then Concord) in New Hampshire. While the Indians were asleep or drunk, likely both, Mrs. Dustin, the child's nurse, and a small boy killed and scalped ten of their twelve captors. Today a monument marks the spot of Hannah Dustin's action.

Rebekah Taylor

Many captives were not as fortunate or as resolute as Hannah Dustin. After her return from captivity Rebekah Taylor told this story to Samuel Penhallow, who recorded it in his history of the Indian wars.

> That when she was going to Canada, on the back of Montreal river, she was violently insulted by Sampson, her bloody master, who without any provocation was resolved to hang her; and for want of a rope, made use of his girdle, which when he had fastened about her neck, attempted to hoist her up on a limb of a tree (that hung in the nature of a gibbet,) but in hoisting her, the weight of her body broke it asunder, which so exasperated the cruel tyrant that he made a second attempt, resolving that if he failed in that to knock her on the head; but before he had power to effect it, Bomaseen came along, who seeing the tragedy afoot, prevented the fatal stroke.

Bomaseen was a sachem of the Kennebecs and one of the fiercest Indian leaders in the onslaught on New England.

Exeter

Hampton was struck by thirty Indians on Tuesday, August 17, 1703. They slew four besides the Widow Mussey who, Penhallow says, "was a remarkable speaking Quaker, and much lamented by that sect." The Indians were no respecters of various creeds among those they considered the heathen English. One Quaker was at a meeting of the Society of Friends when two of his children were killed and scalped. His wife and three other children, one just two weeks old, were stolen to be sold in Canada. The wife and two of the children later escaped, but the oldest daughter was converted and married a French Catholic.

Hampton was attacked several more times, but Exeter, more exposed, was struck again and again.

A company of Mohawks had been lurking about the garrison of Captain Hilton there. When the men went to the fields with scythes to mow, the Indians waited until they had laid down their arms, then killed four, wounded one, and took three captives. As they were dragged to Canada, these captives had nothing to eat for three weeks except a few lily roots and the bark of trees.

Winthrop Hilton, a nephew of Governor Dudley of Massachusetts Bay, was a fearless Indian fighter known, as one writer phrased it, for "his *sharp black eye* and his *long bright gun*." He was a colonel by 1710, when with seventeen men he went to peel the bark from some great trees that had been felled for masts. The Indians ambushed them, took two of the men captive, and killed three, including Colonel Hilton, who had been marked for slaughter. Through surprise and finding their guns wet, the other white men fled without firing a shot. Triumphant at having killed an important enemy, the Indians scalped Hilton, struck their hatchets into his head, and drove a lance into his heart.

Parleys

Occasionally there was a short-lived truce or an uneasy peace. At one point three sachems, Manxis, Wanungonet, and Assacombuit, asked for a parley at Casco with a Major March. When he went forward to greet them, they returned his welcome by drawing hatchets from under their mantles and attacking him. Other Indians in ambush killed one of his guards, but March, a man of uncommon strength, seized a hatchet from one of his assailants and drove them off.

On receiving news of peace between England and France, delegates of the Norridgewock, Narrahamagock (Rocameca), Pennacook, Pequawket, and other tribes came to Portsmouth on July 11, 1713. They asked to be friends and subjects of England's queen. They signed their marks to a lengthy document in which they confessed to their misdeeds and promised never to do it again—but of course, they did. Counselors of both New Hampshire and Massachusetts Bay signed along with Bomaseen, Aeneas, Jackoid, Joseph, Iteansis, and Wadacanaquin.

Delegates of the six nations of the Iroquois, together with Mohegan and Scatacook Indians, met with the General Assembly in Boston a few years later and were sumptuously entertained. They were given many gifts, presented with an ox, which they killed with arrows and dressed, shown a repeating gun that had been invented in Boston as a threat, and promised £100 for the scalp of every enemy Indian, as a bribe for their own good behavior.

Father Sébastien Rale, S.J.

Sébastien Rale (sometimes spelled "Ralle" or "Rasleé") was born in Pontarlier in France in 1654 or 1657. He became a Jesuit priest, volunteered for missionary work in Canada, and sailed in July 1689, in the same ship as the Comte de Frontenac, who was returning for a second term as governor of Canada.

Rale learned Indian dialects while working with settlements near Quebec, then went to Indian villages on the Illinois River. He was recalled in 1693 to be the missionary at Norridgewock, an Abnaki village at St. Francis on the Kennebec, and was joyously received by the Catholic Indians, who attended his services devoutly. According to Cotton Mather, as quoted by Herbert Milton Sylvester in his *Indian Wars of New England*, the French made many Indians believe that Christ was a Frenchman and the Virgin Mary a Frenchwoman.

After a visit to France, Rale returned to St. Francis. He beautified his chapel. He trained a boys' choir. He made altar candles out of bayberry wax. He converted whole tribes of Indians. Belknap says, "He was a man of good sense, learning, and address, and by a compliance with their mode of life, and a gentle, condescending deportment, had gained their affections so as to manage them at his pleasure."

The St. Francis Indians were particularly vicious raiders. They murdered and pillaged year after year in Maine, New Hampshire, and the border towns of Massachusetts Bay. Father Rale encouraged them in their depredations. He made the offices of devotion of the church an incentive to holy war. He gave his charges absolution before they started on a raid and hoisted a flag on which the cross was surrounded by bows and arrows.

Attacks on Norridgewock

Repeatedly Massachusetts Bay urged the French authorities to recall or dismiss Father Rale. The French not only refused but instead ordered him to increase his encouragement of the raids on New England. In the eyes of the English, Rale was a fiend. A price was put on his head, and several times small expeditions were sent to capture or kill him. An English force burned Norridgewock and its chapel in 1705. A party under Colonel Thomas Westbrook struck again in 1721, but Rale had been warned and escaped. All the New Englanders could do was burn his chapel once more and carry off his Bible, Abnaki dictionary, and other treasures.

A full-scale attack was made in August 1724, when two hundred men in seventeen whaleboats moved on the St. Francis village. On the way they killed Bomaseen and his daughters and took his wife captive. Reaching the village, they lay in ambush, then attacked. The Abnaki who were not killed in the first onslaught fled, some drowning in the rapid Kennebec as they struggled to escape. Rale was at the door of his house loading his gun. Lieutenant Richard Jacques called on him to surrender. When Rale said he would give no quarter and take none, Jacques put a bullet through his skull.

About eighty Indians were killed. As Penhallow tells the story, "The number of the dead which we scalped, were twenty-six, besides Monsieur Ralle the Jesuit, who was a bloody incendiary, and instrumental to most of the mischiefs that were done to us, by preaching up the doctrine of meriting salvation by the destruction of Hereticks. . . . After this, they burnt and destroyed the chapel, canoes, and all the cottages that lay around; they also took four Indians alive, and recovered three captives."

This time the New Englanders found Father Rale's trunk, which was covered with brass plate and secured by two locks. In a cunningly hidden secret compartment they discovered letters sent to Rale by the governor of Canada, ordering him to incite the Indians to war and promising support and rewards.

Effect of the Indian Wars

New Hampshire suffered long and sharply from the Indian wars. Business was disrupted, and the prosperity of the Piscataqua towns destroyed. Population was at a standstill, as it was too dangerous to attempt new settlements, and few wished to come to towns already established. Every incentive was held out to men to enlist in the wars against the French and their fierce allies. Enlistments were for two years. A captain was paid £7 a month; a lieutenant, 4; a sergeant received 50 shillings; a corporal, 45; and a private, 40. The real lure, however, was a bounty of £100 for every Indian scalp.

No inducements were sufficient to obtain and maintain forces powerful enough to wipe out the enemy. The Indians swooped down when least expected. Sometimes heroism, quick-wittedness, and good fortune were all that prevented death or capture.

The men were at work in the fields and only women were in the garrison at Oyster River when it was raided in 1710. Loosening their hair and donning men's hats, the women kept up such a fusillade of musketry that the befooled Indians were driven off.

A woman and a child of four were alone in a house attacked in another place. Instructing the child to overturn chairs and make all the noise possible, the woman kept calling out the names of men known to the Indians as she fired at them. They were convinced that a number of men waited to greet them and retreated.

The Wedding at Wells

There was a big wedding when John Wheelwright's daughter married Elisha Plaisted at Wells in Maine. Guests came from Portsmouth and other New Hampshire towns–as did two hundred uninvited Indians. The ceremony was over and the guests were about to depart when it was discovered that the horses were missing. A number of men, including the bridegroom, rushed out, to be met full face by a volley of Indian musket fire. Some were killed, but Plaisted was captured and held for a ransom of £50 in provisions, clothing, and tobacco.

Superstition played its part in another incident. John Magoon of Exeter dreamed that he was being killed by Indians near his brother's barn. Inevitably he began to haunt the spot, and his dream came true.

When in 1722 a body of thirty-four men under Colonel Harmon came on a larger force of Indians asleep around their fire after a drunken orgy, they also found the hand of a white man on a tree stump. Nearby they found his mangled body, the tongue torn out, the nose cut off. They massacred the sleeping Indians.

In 1724 a volunteer company hunting scalps for the bounty came on three Indians. One they thought to be a natural son of Sébastien Rale, for he appeared to be a person of distinction. He was not Rale's but the son of the Baron de Castine, who had married an Indian and for years had been supplying the Indians with arms. The volunteers killed the young half-breed, who wore a coronet of scarlet fur to which four small bells were attached. His Indians—180 of them by the muster roll which, together with a devotional book, was found on him—were supposed to follow the sound of the bells. His hair, when the scalp was peeled from his skull, proved to be remarkably soft and fine.

Hatred of the Indians

Hatred of the Indians was fired by the bitter experience of families in which men were killed and women and children dragged off to torture or slavery in Canada, even in France. The Indians themselves did all they could to fire this fear and hatred. In intervals of peace it was their engaging habit when food was scarce to visit and beg from families of their victims and to regale the survivors with reports of the torture and death of their relatives and friends. When refused what they demanded or when drunk or angered, they threatened repetition of the worst in future encounters.

CHAPTER SIX

Londonderry and Rumford

In 1684 the English Court of Chancery revoked the 1628 charter of the governor and company of Massachusetts Bay and placed Massachusetts, Maine, New Hampshire, and the Narragansett country of Rhode Island under one colonial authority. Joseph Dudley was made provisional president of this Dominion of New England, but was quickly supplanted by Sir Edmund Andros, who had been royal governor of New York.

Sir Edmund Andros

Andros was made governor and captain general of the entire dominion, with headquarters in Boston. With him he brought British troops, clergymen of the Church of England, and all the pomp and ceremony he could introduce into the Province House. He instituted Anglican services, a sacrilege in Boston, into the Old South Meetinghouse, and he did worse. He declared that the colonists did not own their own land or their homes but that everything belonged to the crown, and he began to collect exorbitant fees and taxes.

Andros ruled absolutely with a council of only fifteen men, among them Robert Mason and Edward Randolph, who were his confidants. Seven councilmen constituted a quorum, and were authorized to make and execute laws. New Hampshire had no Assembly now, thus no elected representatives. Town meetings were permitted only for the purpose of electing local officials.

The uproar in Massachusetts Bay was immediate and prolonged. Weakened by the continual Indian wars, New Hampshire could do little

The Council of the Dominion of New England.

more than endure. Mason claimed its lands for himself; Andros claimed them for England. The New Hampshire people said they owed nothing to Mason and had bought their lands from the Indians. Andros scoffed, saying that Indian deeds were "no better than the scratch of a bear's paw."

In this Andros was right. The Indians had no conception of private ownership of land as the English understood it. Land belonged to the tribe for the use of all. Even when they knew what they were doing, the Indians assumed that in selling land they were just giving the English permission to hunt and fish and perhaps farm on it, as they did themselves. Furthermore, one generation of Indians did not feel itself bound by the bear scratches of its fathers.

Andros was right in little else. Arbitrarily he encroached on powers granted him by the crown, arousing the hatred of the people. Even before official notice of the revolution in England which drove James II to flight in France and brought William of Orange and Mary to the throne, the people of Boston had seized Dudley and Andros, locked them in the royal governor's own fort, then sent them as prisoners to London. Triumphantly, Massachusetts Bay resumed the rights granted under its original charter.

New Hampshire was left with no government at all. By general agreement, it reverted to town governments. This situation lasted for one year, from 1689 to 1690. Then New Hampshire petitioned for readmission to Massachusetts Bay. The need for military and financial support in the Indian wars was the chief reason for the move.

This second union with Massachusetts Bay, with Simon Bradstreet governor of both provinces, lasted for two years, 1690–1692. In 1692 New Hampshire again became an independent royal province. This time it remained so, and the royal province of New Hampshire lasted for eighty-three years, or until New Hampshire declared itself independent of Great Britain.

The Scotch-Irish

Despite the wars, which suspended much of its business and made life uncomfortably insecure in the frontier towns, and despite politics—about which, then as now, the ordinary man and woman did not bother—New Hampshire was slowly pushing into new country. The growth of the province was hastened unexpectedly by a pilgrimage from Great Britain and the founding at one stroke of an entire community in a hitherto undeveloped part of the province. The people and the town they built were to be very important to New Hampshire.

Persecuted as Protestants during the seventeenth century, a large group of Scots, strict Presbyterians, left Argyllshire in Scotland and settled in Ulster in northern Ireland. Even after freedom of religion was allowed in Britain they continued to dissent because they still had to pay taxes to support the English church. In addition, they were tenants on the land, not freeholders as they wished to be.

A young Scotch-Irishman, son of a minister named Holmes, of the Scots community in and around Londonderry in Ireland, visited New Hampshire, liked it, and brought back pleasant reports. His father and three other Presbyterian clergymen, James M'Gregore, William Cornweil, and William Boyd, with a large number of their congregations, decided to emigrate to America. Having sold most of their belongings, they started for New England in five ships.

About a hundred families landed in Boston on August 4, 1718. Twenty more families landed at Casco Bay (Portland) in Maine where, on reaching shore, they assembled and sang the 137th Psalm: "How shall we sing the Lord's song in a strange land?" Both bodies petitioned the Massachusetts Bay General Court for a tract of land for a township. Massachusetts gave the immigrants permission to select six square miles anywhere east of Boston.

The Scotch-Irish explored, and sixteen families selected what was then Nutfield, New Hampshire. The rest had gathered at Haverhill, Massachusetts. The men left their families there, examined Nutfield, and built a few houses—really huts—on each side of what they named West-running Brook. Three men remained on guard while the others returned to bring their families from Haverhill.

The First Settlers

These Scots who had lived in Ireland were educated and stouthearted. Some of them were scholars, some skilled artisans. They brought many household furnishings with them and soon had the comforts and even some of the luxuries of civilization in their wilderness. They introduced the art of manufacturing linen of superior quality in America, having brought both the materials and the first spinning wheels operated by foot treadles to be seen in New England.

The M'keen, Barnett, Clendenin, Mitchel, Sterrett, Anderson, Alexander, Gregg, Clark, Nesmith, Morrison, Weir, Allison, Steels, and Stuart families came among the first. As soon as they had decided on Nutfield as site, the Scots sent for the Reverend James M'Gregore, who had passed the winter preaching and teaching at Dracut, Massachusetts. M'Gregore came for a grant of land and twenty shillings annually from every lot in town. He preached his first sermon on April 11, 1719, under a large oak, his text (from Isaiah XXXII:2) "And a man shall be as an hiding place from the wind, and a covert from the tempest; as rivers of water in a dry place; as the shadow of a great rock in a weary land."

The first settlers were quickly joined by others. Born in Scotland,

Archibald Stark and his wife came from Ulster in 1720. Their son, John Stark, was born in 1728.

James Rogers, father of Robert Rogers, came to the town when he was twenty-three, and in 1735 he became one of the founders of Dumbarton. One day, dressed in a bearskin, Rogers went to visit a friend, Ebenezer Ayer, who was just returning to camp after a day's hunt. Mistaking Rogers for a bear, Ayer shot and killed him.

Londonderry

When it was found that Massachusetts Bay had no right to the territory it had granted them, the Scots applied to the New Hampshire Assembly and obtained its grant to the land. They also obtained ten square miles of land from Colonel John Wheelwright, which he claimed by right of his family's Indian deed of 1629.

Lieutenant Governor John Wentworth went out of his way to be kind to the community, which had a large number of people by the end of its first year, for these were the kind of sturdy and responsible people New Hampshire wanted.

Some men in Haverhill claimed the land on which the settlement had been built, and they went there with the intention of taking it forcibly. They arrived to find the Scotch-Irish holding a church service around the oak that had been M'Gregore's first pulpit. Impressed by the firm and resolute appearance of the congregation, the Haverhillians changed their minds, their leader concluding, "It is in vain for us to attempt to disturb this people; we shall not succeed, for God is evidently among them."

In June 1722 the new town was incorporated as Londonderry, in remembrance of the place where most of the newcomers had lived in Ireland.

Church and School

That same year the people of Londonderry built their meetinghouse, making it 50 by 45 feet and high enough for the later installation of galleries. In 1723 they built a log schoolhouse, 12 by 16 feet. Two years later they built schoolhouses in each quarter of the town. More Scotch-Irish came from Ireland, and so quickly did Londonderry grow and prosper that its church had 230 communicants by 1725. When the church was enlarged ten years later, 700 attended the dedicatory service.

Every proprietor in Londonderry built a house, settled his family, went to church, sent his children to school, and cultivated three acres of ground. Here men could work in the fields without fear. Alone of the frontier towns in New Hampshire, Londonderry was never attacked by the Indians. When he delivered a centenary sermon there on April 22, 1819, the Reverend Edwin L. Parker said, "It has generally been thought, that it was owing to a correspondence which the Reverend James M'Gregore held with a French officer, then commanding in Canada, and with whom he had resided at the University in Scotland, that the Indians never molested this town–though the neighboring settlements were repeatedly assaulted."

By the time of the American Revolution, Londonderry was second in importance in New Hampshire only to Portsmouth.

The boundaries between New Hampshire and Massachusetts Bay, 1737.

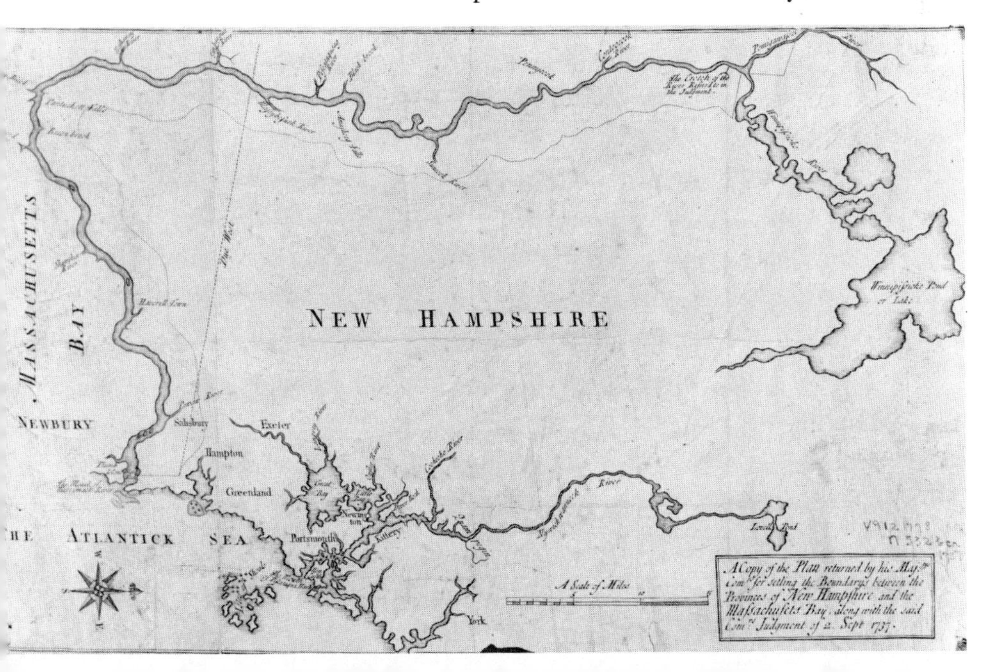

Penacook

On the Merrimack about seventy-five miles northwest of Boston and far removed from the towns along the Piscataqua, Penacook was originally occupied by the Pennacook Indians who, under Passaconaway, were friendly with the English. A trading post was established at Penacook as early as 1660, but there was no real settlement there until 1721. Then the General Court of Massachusetts Bay granted land for a town and sent a hundred chosen families to settle it.

New Hampshire disputed the right of Massachusetts Bay to allocate land that both provinces claimed, and two years later granted the overlapping township of Bow and tried to settle it with Scotch-Irish from Londonderry. A furious dispute ensued, and Massachusetts won the first round. The General Court successfully established its jurisdiction, and what had been Penacook became the Massachusetts township of Rumford.

Rumford

As in the other New Hampshire towns, the settlers of Rumford first threw up huts, then built substantial log cabins, then, as sawmills made lumber available, built houses of from one to three rooms. Two-story homes with stone chimneys and huge fireplaces with ovens and cranes followed. Houses were really built around their fires. Every family had its flint, steel, and tinderbox in case the fire went out. At night pitch pine knots tossed into the fire gave a clear and brilliant light.

Schools were established and children attended them from October 20 to April 20, but, unlike Londonderry, Rumford was vulnerable to Indian attack. A garrison was built around the house of the Reverend Timothy Walker, Rumford's first minister, and the settlers spent the nights within its protective walls of hewn logs. During the day the men went out to the fields in armed companies and placed guards to watch while the others worked.

On the Sabbath all men went armed to church and stacked their guns around a post in the center of the room. The minister preached and prayed with his own fine weapon at his side in the pulpit. Four people were slain in an Indian raid on Rumford in 1746.

The Reverend Timothy Walker

Called the Father of the Town, Timothy Walker was portly, dignified, and greatly respected. He wore a large wig under his three-cornered hat and large silver buckles on his shoes. Exact and precise, he also had a quick temper, which he usually managed to keep under control. He was Rumford's minister and foremost citizen for over half a century.

Timothy Walker used the Westminster Catechism but called himself a moderate Calvinist, and he was not easily carried away by popular pressures. When he was asked to preach on witchcraft, he told his parishioners that the most they had to fear from witches came from talking about them. If they would stop their talk and leave the witches alone, the witches would soon disappear. One instance shows the regard in which the doughty minister, who lived almost until the end of the Revolution, was held. Once when he was away, a group of Indians called at his home, as they often did. Seeing that his wife was fearful, they gave her all their guns, saying they would call for them the next day. They did as they promised.

Walker did not approve of the religious revivalism that swept through Rumford, as through Londonderry, Portsmouth, and all New England, in the 1740's, but it did not need his approval to carry town after town and most of the countryside in between.

George Whitefield

"The Great Awakening," as it was called, originated in Northampton, Massachusetts, under the preaching of the great Jonathan Edwards. It spread across the American colonies through the evangelical enthusiasm of the spellbinding George Whitefield. Whitefield was born in Gloucester in England, was educated at Oxford, and became a disciple of John and Charles Wesley. He first came to America in 1739 and, as he had done in England, mesmerized huge congregations into paroxysms of religious fervor.

Whitefield made religion an emotional rather than a theological matter, and those who heard him soared into transports of ecstasy and religious intoxication. All classes succumbed to his compelling evangelicism which—at first—enthralled the authorities in Boston, the scholars at Harvard, and in Philadelphia even the cynical Benjamin Franklin. Along with the conservative clergy, who looked askance at the theatrics and finally denied Whitefield their pulpits, the Reverend Timothy Walker distrusted the emotional excesses of the Great Awakening.

"Go ye into all the world, and preach the gospel to every creature" (Mark XVI:15) was Whitefield's message, and he did as he adjured. Thirteen times he crossed the Atlantic, and the power to move multitudes never failed him. When he visited Londonderry, even the stern Presbyterians fell under his spell. There, as he did in other places, he preached to huge crowds in an open field. Special prayer meetings and revival services created great excitement.

When George Whitefield died of asthma in September 1770, a horseman galloped into Portsmouth like Paul Revere, crying, "Mr. Whitefield is dead! He died this morning at Newbury, about six o'clock."

Whitefield was buried beneath the First Presbyterian Church of Newburyport, and bells tolled from 11 A.M. to sunset on the day of his funeral.

New Hampshire Victory

If the Reverend Timothy Walker distrusted the Great Awakening, he also distrusted New Hampshire. The dispute with Massachusetts Bay over possession of Rumford waxed fiercely. The whole question of the southern boundary of New Hampshire was a celebrated colonial land dispute. Commissions appointed to investigate and decide reached no clear decisions. Finally the king in council announced in 1741 "that the northern boundary of Massachusetts be a similar curved line pursuing the course of the Merrimack river at three miles distance, on the north side thereof, beginning at the Atlantic ocean and ending at a point due north of Pawtucket Falls; and a straight line drawn from thence due west, till it meet with His Majesty's other governments." The "other governments" would be New York.

This royal decision gave New Hampshire far more land than it had claimed, and it gave it Rumford, which had considered itself part of

Massachusetts. Rumford was displeased and angry. Three times it sent the Reverend Timothy Walker and Benjamin Rolfe to England with petitions that the town be allowed to remain in Massachusetts Bay. Rumford also petitioned the General Court to remain in Massachusetts.

Concord

The petitions were denied, and all attempts to reverse the decision of 1741 failed. Whether it liked it or not, Rumford was a New Hampshire town and a vigorous one. It produced tough fighters for the French and Indian War, and as the Revolution approached, Timothy Walker urged men of the town to fight for independence. Rumford even produced a nobleman of the Holy Roman Empire (see p. 143)—and Joseph Wheat.

An early stage driver, Wheat had a long nose. He told people that when they saw his nose coming they could expect the stage in ten minutes. Once on a cold day when he entered a tavern and sat down to eat, his nose was running. A fastidious patron indignantly told him to wipe it. Wheat looked up at him and said, "Wipe it off yourself, if you please, sir—you are the nearest to it."

Despite these contributions to New England history and folklore, Rumford could not, as it wished, stay in Massachusetts. Instead Rumford became Concord, New Hampshire, in 1765, and was incorporated as Concord in 1784. The first New Hampshire legislature met in Concord in 1782, and the convention to ratify the Federal Constitution was held there in 1788.

CHAPTER SEVEN

People and Customs

Rich men with fine houses, servants, and a few slaves lived in the provincial capital of Portsmouth. These men, merchants most of them, had strong business, political, and social connections in England and often went there. Their ships sailed to Europe, to the West Indies, and down the coast to Boston and the southern ports carrying valuable cargoes each way. The sons of these men were educated at Harvard, then took their places in the governing military and civilian class of New Hampshire.

Shipbuilding

There were also sailors, longshoremen, and artisans in all the trades having to do with the sea in and around Portsmouth. Shipbuilding was carried on all along the lower Piscataqua and its branches. New Hampshire had skilled ships' carpenters, and there was sound wood for the hulls and for the finest white-pine masts available anywhere. Fishing schooners and whaleboats were often built two or three miles inland, then hauled to the sea. Big ships were usually built at the shore, but some were constructed a mile or two inland; then as many as two hundred oxen drew them on strong sleds over the snow onto the river ice. When the ice melted in the spring, the ships were floated down to the sea.

For eighty years the British navy got all of its white-pine masts from America, some of the best from New Hampshire. It also got some of its fighting ships there, as did the united colonies at a later period. All of these warships were built at Portsmouth:

Faulkland	54 guns	1690	
Bedford	32 "	1696	
America	40 "	1749	
Raleigh	72 "	1776	
Ranger	18 "	1777	(for John Paul Jones)
America	74 "	1782	(presented to the King of France by the Continental Congress)

Religion

Important families of the governing class in New Hampshire remained loyal to the Church of England. The Reverend Arthur Browne, a native of Ireland, who took his master's degree at Trinity College in Dublin in 1729, was ordained as a missionary to Providence, Rhode Island. In 1736 he was inducted as rector of the Episcopal church in Portsmouth. The Society for the Propagation of the Gospel in London paid him £60 a year and another £15 for services he conducted in Kittery, across the river in Maine. The parish paid the rest of his £100 a year salary, which was large for the time.

Other families attended the Puritan, or Congregational, churches or, because of the tolerance that characterized New Hampshire, whatever church they chose or none at all. Most people in the smaller towns went to church. Even if it was not obligatory, church going was customary. It was the great social gathering of the week. Most people walked to meeting, some of them six or seven miles. Farmers usually rode on horseback, their wives on pillions behind them. Church services were Sabbath-long, with the intervals between the lengthy morning and afternoon sermons and psalm singing free for the weekly exchange of news and gossip.

Food

New Hampshire is cold country, the growing season short, but its people ate heartily in the seventeenth and eighteenth centuries. There was always plenty of game; venison and wild birds were available cheaply in the markets as well as free in the woods and fields. Increas-

The kitchen of the Captain John Clark House shows the typical domestic arrangements of a New Hampshire dwelling in the mid-1700's. The cavernous fireplace with a brick oven at the back provided all the facilities for cooking that the housewife needed.

ing herds of cattle provided meat besides milk, cream, and butter. From the Indians the settlers had learned how to raise corn, beans, pumpkins, and squash—and to plant corn when the leaves of the white oak were as big as the ear of a mouse. The Indians, who taught the English the medicinal values of various herbs, roots, and bark, also taught them early about their version of quick-frozen foods—that is, filling the hollows of dressed poultry with snow and then packing them in casks of snow—as well as how to preserve meats by smoking them.

Eaten throughout the northern colonies, succotash was not just corn and beans but more like a rich stew, with many vegetables and often meat. Hasty pudding, made of cornmeal, seasoning, and water or milk, was standard fare. In New Hampshire breakfast was usually bean or pea porridge, eaten with wooden spoons from a wooden bowl. It was delicious. There was always bread of rye and Indian meal, and at breakfast on Sunday there was coffee or chocolate.

Dinner, always at midday, was baked or boiled meat, peas or beans, and pudding. The Londonderry Scotch-Irish introduced potatoes and potato growing, thus adding to the menu. In the coast towns there were, of course, plenty of saltwater fish, and the rivers and lakes everywhere provided trout, salmon, bass, and other freshwater fish in profusion. A luxury dish in New Hampshire was baked pumpkin. A pumpkin was filled with milk and well cooked, then allowed to stand for twelve hours or more. After that more milk was added, and then the pumpkin was eaten with a spoon right out of its shell.

Drink

If New Hampshire colonists ate well, they drank thirstily. Beer, the drink of the Puritans and Pilgrims, was soon superseded by cider, because hops did not grow well in New Hampshire. Families drank cider at every meal, and when the apples were pressed in the fall, laid in a store of from fifteen to thirty barrels for the year, sometimes much more. Nathaniel Bouton in his *History of Concord* says that the town possessed some noted cider topers, who begged a quart at the door, then downed it without stopping for breath. They were easily recognized, he says, for they had "a bloated, red face and pot-belly."

Cider was the common drink among farmers, and in some frontier towns there was another drink of spruce twigs boiled in maple sap; but wines and hard liquor were enthusiastically imbibed by all classes, especially in the lumber regions and in the Piscataqua fishing, shipping, and shipbuilding towns. The wealthy had glittering displays of fine wines and spirits on their sideboards. The magistrates and gentry drank wine and brandy at home and at their meetings, which were frequently held in taverns. The tavern keeper was an important man in the community. Samuel Wentworth owned the Dolphin Inn on Great Island, a place that was busy with sail and crowded with sailors. Later he built a larger and much frequented tavern in Portsmouth.

Much of the revenue of New Hampshire came from tariffs on liquor and from fees paid by those licensed to sell drink. Wines were imported from the Azores, the Canary Islands, and Spain, rum from Jamaica. Every store had a liquor counter, and few neglected the rum, brandy, wines, and gin sold at it. Men drank hard liquor flavored with spearmint, tansy, or garden wormwood as an appetizer before breakfast.

Farmers carried bottles of rum with them all winter and took them into the fields in the summer. Bouton says that the liquor consumption in Rumford was four and a half gallons a year for every man, woman, and child.

In Rumford in 1762 the principal store was kept by Andrew McMillan. His bills to the principal people of the town showed large purchases of wine, brandy, and rum. In January 1762, the Reverend Timothy Walker bought brandy and rum by the gallon and half gallon. He bought several more gallons of rum in December. His deacons were just as thirsty, and Rumford's doctor—who may have dispensed some of it to his patients—bought half gallons of rum on eight different occasions in the one month of January 1763. There is no telling, of course, how much more liquor these gentlemen obtained from other sources, or how much beer and cider they used to wash down the rum.

Flip was a favorite tavern drink. It was made by sweetening malt beer with sugar, thrusting in a hot iron to produce foam, and adding rum—a half pint to a quart mug, which sold for from twenty to twenty-five cents. Another favorite, toddy, consisted of sweetened rum and water.

Dress

The wealthy could and did buy and wear fine silks, satins, and velvets imported from England. They dressed when they could in the newest London fashions. Portsmouth was a provincial capital, smaller than Boston, but like it in formality and polite manners among the elite. Gentlemen in wigs and fine raiment were as colorful as their ladies in silken gowns, elaborate jewelry, high heels, and towering coiffures.

Ordinary men and women wore homespun garments made by the women of the family from flax and wool they had spun and woven themselves. Generally men wore a woolen coat, a smock or waistcoat of stripped wool or tow (hemp or flax), and woolen, velvet, or leather breeches. Their long stockings were tucked inside tight breeches, which were fastened at the knee, sometimes with buckles, sometimes with buttons. In winter they wore thick cowhide shoes fastened with buckles and sometimes woolen or leather buskins reaching halfway to the knee.

In summer women wore long-skirted, full-sleeved tow or linen gowns and checked aprons. In winter the gowns and aprons were of wool. A story, which may or may not be true, is told of their skill and speed in fashioning clothes for their families. When the Reverend Jacob Emery of Pembroke was summoned to a meeting of the Provincial Congress to be held at Exeter the following day, he discovered that his wardrobe did not contain breeches befitting either his dignity or the occasion. So a sheep was caught and clipped, and his wife carded, spun, and wove the wool. She designed and made the pantaloons in time for him to set out before dawn the next day—enabling her minister husband to appear properly in sheep's clothing.

Diversions

Of necessity New Hampshire's people were industrious. Hard work was the rule, but they did find time for play.

In the larger towns there were formal assemblies for dancing, and theatrical entertainments were performed by gentlemen and ladies. The various governors and their coteries had their receptions and levees. In Portsmouth, society never observed all the Puritan restrictions, nor did lesser people. Young men and women danced at military musters, ship launchings, the ordination of ministers, and other celebrations.

In the smaller towns and the farming communities there was much visiting back and forth. Women took their babies with them to afternoon socials—baby-sitters had not yet been invented—where they visited, sewed, and quilted. Afterward they prepared a supper at which they were joined by the men for pies and doughnuts, sometimes roast meat or turkey, with cider for the men and tea for the women. Usually there was dancing after supper. The festivities broke up early, as everyone had to face morning chores.

Corn huskings and harvest time justified festivities and merriment. Target shooting was a regular and useful pastime for men and boys, and at Christmas there were shooting matches for geese at which wagers were made.

House or barn raisings often ended with a wrestling match, the shouting crowd placing bets on their favorites. The matches were sometimes between local combatants, but there were wrestlers whose fame carried farther, and they often journeyed considerable distances to test their skill against one another. One wrestler noted for his prowess heard of the strength and skill of John McNeil of Londonderry and could not resist the challenge to his reputation. He appeared at the McNeil home with the announced intention of throwing the Londonderry champion. The story is that McNeil was away at the time but that his wife hospitably did not wish the challenger, who had come many miles, to be disappointed, so she suggested that she wrestle him herself. At first the stranger was reluctant, but she taunted him into agreement. The wrestler accepted the challenge and quickly found himself flat on his back. The discomfited athlete did not wait for John McNeil's return.

Disputes

New Hampshire men and women loved their neighbors but not all of them and not all the time.

Brawls between husbands and wives and quarrels among neighbors were commonplace. Fisticuffs sprang out of disagreements and dislikes, possibly boredom. The courts were busy with plaintiffs hotly accusing defendants of bodily harm or slander and with defendants just as hotly protesting their own innocence and the guilt of their accusers.

In Portsmouth two sailors testified that about midnight on October 1, 1685, a certain Thomas Parker sent a boy of whom he was master to find his paddles. Instead, the boy, who had been beaten, hid himself in a pigsty. When he was discovered, he ran out into the river. There one Joseph Alexander caught him and ducked him five or six times while Parker cried out, "Drown the dog!" A Portsmouth joiner also testified on the boy's behalf.

In another case, a woman was in one canoe and a man in another. He drove her ashore and struck her several blows on the head, swearing, that by God, he would be the death of her. She ran off, and another woman dressed her broken head.

On November 3, 1685, a merchant of Boston took oath that a certain Abrabram Lee of Cochecho had threatened to kill him. Since he did not want to be killed, he begged the court to make Lee cease and desist.

Constables were continually being ordered in His Majesty's name to attach the goods or, in want of goods, the body, of some miscreant and either take his bond or throw him into jail.

Education

Because New Hampshire was a part of Massachusetts Bay for almost forty years after 1641, it was subject to the same laws concerning education, and Massachusetts gave early attention to this subject, which it considered of prime importance. The Boston Latin School was founded in 1634, Harvard College by the General Court in 1636. In 1647 Massachusetts Bay passed its famous "Old Deluder" act. To foil the Devil, or Old Deluder, who thrives on ignorance, this act provided that every town of fifty families hire a schoolmaster to teach its children to read and write, and that every town of one hundred families establish a grammar school (i.e., high school or academy) to prepare youth for the university.

In both Massachusetts Bay and New Hampshire, most towns that were able readily complied, but in both provinces some towns could not or would not do it. As a rule, the common school was built and manned, and children learned their reading, writing, and 'rithmetic. Portsmouth itself appropriated considerable sums annually for the support of Harvard, but many of the smaller towns neglected even to set up grammar schools.

Jeremy Belknap puts the case with his usual insight.

> When the leading men in a town were themselves persons of knowledge and wisdom, they would provide the means of instruction for children; but where the case was otherwise, methods were found to evade the law. The usual way of doing this was to engage some person to keep a school for a few weeks before the court term, and discontinue it soon after. It was to the interest of ignorant and unprincipled men to

> discourage literature; because it would detract from their importance, and expose them to contempt. The people in some places being thus misled, thought it better to keep their children at work, than provide for their instruction.

Note that Belknap says children were kept "at work," not "at home" or "at play." Colonial families were large, and second and third marriages were general. Widows of men killed in the various wars remarried quickly; widowers remarried just as promptly. Boys from these large families were put to work on farms at a very young age or apprenticed to craftsmen in the various trades.

Slavery

Negro slavery never thrived in New Hampshire or in New England generally. It was opposed from the first, although New England sea captains were often involved in the slave trade. In 1645 when a Negro was brought from the coast of Africa and sold, he was taken from his master by order of the court and returned to his home in Africa. Gradually the prohibition was relaxed, and some Negro slaves entered the province, but they were few.

The real slavery in colonial New Hampshire was of Indians, captured, enslaved, and sold abroad or in the South—and of white English slaves, men and women captured by Indians and sold in Canada or shipped to France. For centuries slaves had been considered part of the spoils of war. Wars were fought in Europe for the express purpose of obtaining white slaves. Christian whites were enslaved in North Africa, where Morocco had an infamous slave mart. The General Court of Massachusetts Bay passed laws against the buying or selling of slaves, except those "taken in lawful war, or reduced to servitude for their crimes by a judicial sentence."

Some of the wealthy families in the Piscataqua towns had Negro slaves for house servants. There were a few in Rumford in the mid-eighteenth century. One, named in the bill of sale as Boy Caesar, died at the age of ninety-two. A Negro girl named Dinah married and settled in nearby Canterbury. Aaron Stevens, called Crowner, was the

Rumford dog whipper. His job was to keep dogs out of the meeting-house, a task for which he was paid small sums. Abraham Bradley bought Pompey for thirty bushels of corn. Pompey became a family favorite and a bodyguard for Bradley's son. When the son died, Bradley left Pompey the use of a half acre of land near his home.

According to the historian McClintock, the total number of "Negroes and Slaves for life" (the latter probably Indians and convicted criminals) in New Hampshire in 1767 was 633. By 1775 there were only 479. All slaves were freed on adoption of the Federal Constitution, though some dreaded this. Bouton tells the story of Nancy, for whom Lieutenant Richard Herbert paid five dollars when she was about eighteen months old. Nancy was sent to school with the children of his family and treated like one of them. When the New Hampshire constitution was adopted in 1783, Nancy, fearing she might be returned to Boston, her place of birth, burst into tears.

The rest of the family gathered around her and assured her that she was to remain in what had always been her home. Nancy became an esteemed member of the Concord church with a particular interest in foreign missions. She left bequests for this work in her will when she died at the age of seventy-nine.

Longevity

All four of the original New Hampshire settlements were maritime. There was the usual licentiousness of port towns anywhere. Sex offenses were commonplace; smuggling was universal; piracy, called privateering during the wars, was general and profitable. That was part of it all.

New Hampshire also had its shrewd traders, and they grew rich. It had skilled workmen. It had men who knew how to swing an ax in the woods, and others who could handle ox teams. Horses were seldom used for hauling, only for riding and for pulling sleighs in the winter. Especially in the outlaying towns, which were really only small clearings in a vast wilderness, life was hard and demanding. It developed strong men and women—for only the rugged survived.

Many lived a long time. Middle-aged when they came from Ulster, many of the original settlers of Londonderry lived into their late eighties, some into their nineties. William Scooby lived to be 110. In Dover, Howard Henderson, who died in 1722, was 100. In Durham a preacher named John Buss died in 1736, aged 108. William Perkins died in Newmarket at 116. Robert Mackin, an intrepid Scot who lived in Portsmouth, often walked from there to Boston, sixty-six miles, in one day and returned the next—at least Belknap says he did. Macklin gave this up when he was eighty; he died at 115.

As in Boston and other provincial capitals, the funerals of wealthy or prominent men in Portsmouth were elaborate and expensive before the Revolution. In Portsmouth all the relatives of the deceased were required to dress in full suits of mourning. Enameled rings were distributed to near relatives and close friends, and gloves and rings were given to the pallbearers and the clergy. Often the family's armorial bearings were painted on silk, then laid on the coffin, hung over the door, and sent to friends. When hard times came with the Revolution, these elaborate mourning customs gave way to simpler ones. Then men simply wore bands of black crepe on their left sleeves, and women wore black ribbons in token of grief at bereavement.

Fighting Men

All New Hampshire men under forty were subject to military service in the provincial militia. They had known how to handle guns from boyhood. They had their training days and went through the drills, but many had no wish to be soldiers. They were needed on their farms, particularly at planting or harvest time, or they had a trade, a shop or tavern, or a political post to protect.

Other men welcomed military duty and sought it, and from these New Hampshire developed its own breed of fighting men. Hunters, trappers, and timbermen—men of the frontier, hard and adventurous—preferred the woods, rivers, and lakes to life in the towns. Crack shots, they lived on game or, when none was to be found, on salt pork and beef. They guzzled rum, plenty of it, when they could get it, or they made do with ginger and water. A hut or lean-to did them for shelter, or they went without and, wrapped in a blanket, slept on the ground, their feet to the fire, sometimes in subzero weather.

When unemployed, these men frequented the taverns and disported themselves as best they could, but they were happiest testing their skill, endurance, and courage against the wiliest of adversaries. They had learned the guerrilla tricks of the Indians and could move as silently through the forests and with as deadly a purpose. Almost professionals, they were uneasy in the brief intervals of peace.

New Hampshire had needed such men from its beginnings. It continued to need them.

CHAPTER EIGHT

The French and Indian War

The heirs of John Mason, the founder and original proprietor of New Hampshire, kept up the fight to regain what legally and ethically they considered theirs, but it was a losing fight. New Hampshire had grown away from the ideas of its first owners. A generation that had never known Captain John Mason or life in England under landlords held tenaciously to the properties they had developed and maintained.

Governor Samuel Allen and Lieutenant Governor John Usher

Crown decisions and court judgments might favor Robert Tufton Mason, but they were thwarted by every possible means, legal and illegal. Robert Mason died in Esopus, New York, in 1688, leaving two sons, John and Robert. They had no desire to live in New Hampshire or to take up what must have seemed to them a hopeless cause. By a deed of April 27, 1691, they sold the entire province to Samuel Allen, a London merchant, for £2,750, so at least they got something back on their great-grandfather's outlay.

The next year Allen got himself appointed governor of New Hampshire, and his son-in-law, John Usher, a Boston merchant, as lieutenant governor. This meant that Usher, who was on the scene, was the *de facto* governor.

Usher tried his best, for there was money to be made, but he found himself flouted at every turn. In New Hampshire, records which would have substantiated his case were conveniently missing. He found himself consistently opposed by the wealthy and powerful Wentworths and their connections in Portsmouth. They forced him out of office and got their own man, William Partridge, appointed lieutenant governor in 1697.

In a countermove Usher persuaded his father-in-law to come to New England himself and assume his governorship of New Hampshire. Allen came in 1698 and restored his deputy to the lieutenant governorship. The move failed, for when the Earl of Bellemont was made royal governor of New York, Massachusetts Bay, and New Hampshire in 1699, the Wentworth-sponsored William Partridge went back in as lieutenant governor of the province.

John Usher had one more chance when he became lieutenant governor under Joseph Dudley, but succeeded no better on this third attempt than he had on the first two. The lawsuits, judgments, and counteractions kept on with no result. If the date of 1623 is taken as a starting point, the Mason claims were prosecuted for 139 years. They came to a conclusive end in 1762 when England's famed chief justice, Lord Mansfield, handed down a decision in London which said, in effect, that natural right lies at the foundation of legal right and is to be maintained against biased judgments based on legal technicalities.

One reason for the thwarting, then the final defeat, of the Mason-Allen-Usher claims was that during those years New England, particularly New Hampshire, had more pressing matters to attend to. Dominant among them was the continuing bitter struggle with the French and their Indian allies.

Lovewell's War

The depredations of the Indians were keeping New Hampshire thin and poor. Characteristically it was a war of sporadic and isolated raids, murder, pillage, arson, the capturing of prisoners—with the English on the defensive. What has become known in verse, ballads, and stories as "Lovewell's War" was different. This time the colonists went on the offensive, took the conflict into the White Mountains, which were at least partway in enemy territory, and faced the raiders in a pitched battle.

John Lovewell was born October 14, 1689, in that part of Dunstable, Massachusetts, which became Nashua, New Hampshire. His father had served under Captain Benjamin Church in the Great Swamp Fight in which King Philip had been hunted down and killed. Lovewell was a farmer, married, and the father of two children when the Indians attacked Dunstable. With a few other men Lovewell petitioned the General Court for a commission to range the woods, hunt down, and destroy the hit-and-run Indians. The court agreed to pay two and a half shillings per day per man and a bounty of £100 for each Indian scalp.

In December 1724, Lovewell with thirty men killed one Indian and captured a boy. The following February with eighty-seven men he scouted along the Merrimack River past Lake Winnipesaukee into the White Mountain region. This time they surprised and killed ten sleeping Indians. Triumphantly, on March 10, 1725, they marched through Dover with the scalps aloft on poles. In Boston they collected the £1000 bounty.

On a third expedition Lovewell with forty-six men marched on the stronghold of the Pequawkets near Fryeburg, Maine. At Lake Ossipee, New Hampshire, he built a small fort and left some of his men to garrison it. Then with thirty-four men Lovewell crossed the Saco River. The Indians were ready. Decoyed by one Indian who deliberately let himself be seen, Lovewell and his force were ambushed. Lovewell and several others were killed by a volley of musket fire.

The survivors dropped their packs and retreated to take shelter behind trees near the shore of what, ever since, has been called Lovewell's Pond. By counting the packs, the forty-one Indians—a war party on its way to capture colonists—knew that they outnumbered the enemy. Lovewell's men knew this too, but, backed against the water, they began a fierce battle which lasted from the middle of the forenoon until almost dark that evening.

The well-armed Indians barked like dogs and howled like wolves as they fired. Lovewell's men responded with shouts and huzzas. Paugus, sachem of the Indians, called on the beleaguered men to surrender. They refused and continued to fire furiously. Chaplain Jonathan Frye, not long out of Harvard, was mortally wounded but prayed aloud for the others until he died.

The Indians stopped for a ceremonial powwow. Seeing this, Captain Seth Wyman crept up and shot and killed their leader. This deterred the Indians, who carried spare blankets, moccasins, and snowshoes for the prisoners they expected to capture. They withdrew, unable even to carry off their dead.

Only nine of the thirty-four men in Lovewell's army were unhurt. Ensign Robbins, too seriously wounded to move, asked to have a gun left with him so that he could kill one more savage before he died. Then, toward midnight, under a bright moon, the others began the long trek back to the fort at Ossipee. When they reached it, they found that its frightened garrison had fled but had left some bread and pork, which sustained them.

More hardships followed. On their return to Nashua, Wyman and three others were without food from Saturday morning until Wednesday, when they killed and roasted two squirrels. Afterward they found partridge and other game and were well enough fed until they reached home. A search party sent out found the bodies of Lovewell, Robbins, and the others and buried them where they had fallen, carving the names of the twelve English dead on the trees. In a shallow grave they found the bodies of Paugus and two other Indians. The guns with which the French had supplied the Indians were of such high quality that they brought good prices when they were sold in Boston.

Lovewell was killed, and his force suffered badly, but he broke the war spirit of the Pequawkets. The victory, so costly to him and his men, became celebrated. One of Longfellow's first poems was "The Battle of Lovell's Pond." Nathaniel Hawthorne, whose stories of "The Great Stone Face," "The Ambitious Guest," and others are all set in the White Mountains, which so fascinated him, wrote "Roger Malvin's Burial" about two of the survivors of Lovewell's War.

Louisburg

The most spectacular and important event of the bitter war of 1740–1748 was the siege of Louisburg. Known as the "Gibraltar of

America," this French fort, guarding the entrance to the Gulf of the St. Lawrence, was considered impregnable. The entire town, two and a half miles in circumference, was heavily fortified. It was surrounded by a stone rampart 30 to 36 feet high, with a ditch 80 feet wide in front of it. On an island at the entrance to its harbor was a battery of thirty cannon, which carried 28-pound shot. At the bottom of the harbor was a royal battery of twenty-eight 42-pounders and two 18-pound cannon. Entrance to the town was over a drawbridge protected by a circular battery of thirteen 24-pound cannon. The whole had taken France twenty-five years to build at a cost of about $6 million.

Merchant son of the lieutenant governor, William Vaughan of Portsmouth was seized with the idea that Louisburg could be taken by a surprise naval and land assault. He laid his plan before Governor William Shirley of Massachusetts Bay and obtained his quick agreement. Then he rode posthaste back to Portsmouth and presented it to the New Hampshire Assembly. The assembly immediately voted £4,000 for the attack and authorized the governor to raise troops and provide transport, arms and ammunition, and stores.

A united force of colonial troops set out under a slogan given it by the worshiped George Whitefield, *Nil desperandum Christo duce* (freely translated, "All is possible when Christ leads"), which, as the writer McClintock says, gave the expedition "almost the character of a crusade."

Sir William Pepperell

Sir William Pepperell was the great man of Maine. Son of a shipbuilder and trader who accumulated great wealth and a vast estate, Pepperell lived like a lord in a great house in Kittery. It had fine English furniture, china, and plates, a cellar of old wines, and a library, used by ministers and scholars, which was the best in northern New England. The park was stocked with deer. Pepperell had his coach drawn by six horses. Mounted, he could ride for thirty miles toward Portsmouth completely on his own land. His barge was manned by six uniformed slaves. The richest merchant in the country, Pepperell sometimes had as many as two hundred ships at sea. He was reputed to be worth £200,000 sterling.

Despite his awesome riches, Pepperell was popular. He could draw soldiers to him—farmers, mechanics, woodsmen, and fishermen, most of them—and even help pay them. He spent some £5,000 of his own money on the Louisburg campaign. Already a militia colonel, Pepperell was commissioned a lieutenant general and placed in command of the colonial army.

The Siege

In the army when Pepperell's expedition set sail from Nantasket on March 24, 1745, were five hundred New Hampshire men, about one eighth of the total New England force, but ranking higher in percentage of combat troops. The expedition was to rendezvous with ships of the British fleet, but these arrived late. The colonial force had already landed and set up camp at Gabarus Bay on Cape Breton. For nearly three weeks, Pepperell was held up by the ice in Canso Strait.

The French had heard rumors of the coming attack but discounted them. Morale was low in Louisburg, where there were 560 French regulars and about 1,500 militia. The soldiers were mutinous and slow. It took them days to get their batteries into position.

With the British ships bombarding the town and preventing reinforcements and supplies from reaching it, the siege of Louisburg began May 4, 1745. Fired by battle ardor, Lieutenant Colonel William Vaughan of Portsmouth led a force of marauders made up of New Hampshire commandos through the woods directly in sight of the town. He captured and burned warehouses and destroyed a large quantity of liquor. The next day he fought his way into Louisburg itself and, with only thirteen men, seized and held a French battery in the face of fire from a hundred defenders—and he continued to hold it until reinforcements arrived.

New Hampshire men were in the thick of the fight. Later they felt they got insufficient recognition in the dispatches to England. Belknap describes some of their efforts:

They were employed for fourteen nights successively, in drawing cannon from the landing place to the camp, through a morass, and their Lieutenant Colonel Messerve, being a ships carpenter, constructed sledges on which the cannon were drawn, when it was found that their wheels were buried in the mire. The men, with straps over their shoulders, and sinking to their knees in mud, performed labours beyond the power of oxen; which labor could be done only at night or on a foggy day; the place being within plain view and random shot of the enemy's walls.

Yet a prolonged siege can be tedious business. The men labored and fought, but as some who had been there told Belknap laughingly, the siege was carried on like a riotous Cambridge commencement. The ground was uneven, so they knew the French could not estimate their number. There was no discipline; only the popularity of Pepperell held these militiamen from different provinces together. "They indeed," Belknap says, "presented a formidable front to the enemy; but the rear was a scene of confusion and frolic. While some were on duty at the trenches, others were racing, wrestling, pitching quoits, firing at marks, or running after shot from the enemy's guns, for which they received a bounty, and the shot were sent back to the city."

Fall of Louisburg

Pepperell demanded Louisburg's surrender. Its commandant, Du Chambon, refused. Then a 64-gun French warship, the *Vigilant*, sailed straight into the English fleet. The English took her crew of five hundred prisoner, manned the ship with British sailors, and turned her cargo of munitions, intended for the defenders, over to the attackers, who needed and used them.

The cannonading and assault began. About half Pepperell's four thousand men were out of action with wounds or illness. The attackers sent the Marquis de la Maisonforte, the French captain of the captured *Vigilant*, in under a flag of truce to tell Louisburg of his downfall. There were more skirmishes, some with heavy casualties, before Du Chambon asked for a cessation of hostilities. He offered terms, but they were refused. Then Pepperell and Commodore Warren of the British naval squadron agreed on new terms under which the French forces were allowed to march out of the Gibraltar of America with their arms and colors. The New England troops marched into Louisburg.

It was a glorious victory. The French had lost 300 men, the New Englanders only 130 in battle, though more died from exposure. New Hampshire lost five men in combat, six through illness. Pepperell, who was of distinguished appearance and had courtly manners, was feted in London, made a baronet for his achievement, and commissioned a lieutenant general in the royal army.

In American eyes, it was a useless victory, although it made the British Empire ruler by the acquisition of Madras. Louisburg was ceded back to France by the Treaty of Aix-la-Chapelle, which ended this particular war in 1748, and had to be recaptured in the next war.

The French and Indian War

The last and largest of the Indian wars began in 1754. This was more than just one in a series of regional conflicts between New Englanders and raiding Indians. It was a theater of operations in what was, for its time, almost a world war, in which the chief European powers struggled for supremacy. Crack regiments of British troops and a series of major English military commanders, including the ill-fated Edward Braddock, fought in the French and Indian War. In America the British used both land and sea forces in a fight to a decision.

The struggle really began with the revolution in England which unseated James II. The Catholic-versus-Protestant aspect of this war led to the incursions of Catholic Canada into Protestant New England, but more than religious creeds was at stake. Great Britain had its imperialistic plans in the New World, and France had hers. In addition, two different kinds of civilization were in conflict.

France had been in possession of the St. Lawrence valley before the first British settlement was made in New Hampshire. The French had settled there as early as 1610. The population was small, and permanent settlement was difficult to achieve. Under autocratic and feudal rule, the French were fur traders, and Jesuit missionaries were soon active and successful among the natives. Besides trading and converting, the French explored. Marquette, Joliet, and LaSalle penetrated the Mississippi and Ohio valleys. French fur traders extended the influence of France throughout the region of the Great Lakes. Establishing forts and trading posts, not towns, was the way of the mobile and ambitious French.

With Spain an active, though secret, ally, France intended to limit the English to their settlements along the Atlantic coast. The French built a series of strongholds, including forts at Niagara, Detroit, St. Joseph at the southern end of Lake Michigan, and Michilimackinac, which guarded the upper Great Lakes. The conquest and possession of vast territory was what France wanted. On the other hand, England was determined to have no limits set to her colonization. The French and Indian War was a widespread British offensive to make sure no such limits held.

Fort Number 4 was an important defense against the Indians on the Connecticut River frontier of New Hampshire during the colonial period.

George Washington

It was in this war that a young Virginia planter named George Washington was commissioned a lieutenant colonel of the Virginia and North Carolina militia and, in April 1754, set out to drive the French and Indians from the Ohio. At Great Meadows in Pennsylvania he built Fort Necessity, which was quickly surrounded by 1,500 French and Indians. After a nine-hour battle the fort was forced to surrender, Washington signing articles of capitulation on July 4, 1754, and marching his men back to Virginia. This defeat was the real beginning of the French and Indian War.

Washington served under Braddock when in 1755 the major general led 1,400 English regulars and 700 militia from Virginia, Pennsylvania, and the Carolinas against the French at Fort Duquesne (Pittsburgh). His army, marching in strict battle order, was slaughtered by the French, Canadians, and Indians. Sixty-three of Braddock's eighty officers and half his men were killed or wounded. Braddock had four horses shot from under him, one after the other. With bullets in his arm and lungs he died four days later at Great Meadows.

The New Hampshire Border

It was an inauspicious beginning. The enemy rampaged almost unchecked along the whole English frontier. New Hampshire settlements on the Connecticut River were particularly exposed, protected only by Fort Dummer in the southwest corner of the province and by Number 4. This last was a settlement and fort that had been built on the advice of Colonel John Stoddard (uncle of Jonathan Edwards) of Northampton in Massachusetts Bay. It had been settled in 1743 by people from Hadley, Hatfield, Deerfield, and Sunderland. Several times it was attacked but successfully defended against superior enemy forces. Depredations along the Connecticut were continuous, severe, and particularly barbarous. Every house was a garrison. Men came running from the fields at the sound of a horn or a gunshot signal—and usually they were too late.

In his painstakingly detailed *Indian Wars of New England* (1910) Herbert Milton Sylvester says bitterly, if a little rhetorically:

> The Indians were clearly for war; and no compact of peace, however solemnly entered into, was binding upon them. They were thirsty for the blood of the settlers, and in the prosecution of their inclinations had degenerated into a band of midnight plunderers, butchers, and incendiarists. They were beasts of prey. It is a wonder they abstained from cannibalism, such was their delight to glut themselves with the blood of the defenceless and helpless women and children, once they had butchered their natural protectors.

The French paid the Indians well for scalps, more for prisoners. They used captives as articles of commerce, demanding high ransoms or selling them in Canada or France. A whole family, captured at Salisbury in New Hampshire in 1754, was sold in Canada, then shipped to France, but was rescued at sea by an English ship and put ashore at Portsmouth. Eunice Garfield, captured at Hinsdale, was sold and sent to France but escaped to England, got back to Boston, and lived to be eighty-seven. In Walpole, Colonel Bellows, one of the town's first settlers, fought his way with only twenty men through two hundred Indians to the shelter of the garrison. In 1755 in the same town John Kilburn fought off two hundred Indians with a force of three men and two women.

Even the Indians, though, learned to fear one group of fighters. Sylvester says, and his words have been echoed by other writers, "The savages were chary about meeting New Hampshire men, who had gained a reputation not only of being hardy and agile, but also of being expert backwoodsmen whose guns were fatal."

Robert Rogers

New Hampshire provided its share of militiamen who fought with the British regulars, but its chief and most effective contribution to the French and Indian War was a new kind of soldier under a new kind of leader.

Of Londonderry Scotch-Irish parentage, Robert Rogers was born in 1731 in Methuen, Massachusetts, but grew up—grew to be a giant in stature, tall, heavy, and almost indestructible—on his father's farm near

Major Robert Rogers

Rumford. He became a woodsman, a hunter, and, very early, an Indian fighter. At nineteen he was already a scout under Captain Ladd in the Merrimack valley; three years later he was on the same duty for Captain Ebenezar Eastman of Penacook. The big young man could move through the forest as silently as the foe he stalked. He knew Indians and their habits, and he was a better shot than most of them. In January 1755, he recruited men for Governor William Shirley's expedition against Canada. Then, supposedly to escape prosecution for counterfeiting the currency of the province, he joined a New Hampshire regiment. Robert Rogers' boldness in scouting and leading scouts led Shirley to appoint him captain of an independent company of Rangers.

Rogers' Rangers were picked men, each one a woodsman and a hunter, tough-fibered and strong, who could fight like the Indians. The Rangers were on their own as a company, and when the situation required it, each man was on his own as a self-sufficient fighter. The Rangers wore green uniforms, stout shoes or moccasins, leggings, coarse smallclothes, and a warm, close-fitting tam (Tam-o'-shanter) or beret. Each man carried a hatchet in his belt, a rifle, a powder horn, a hunting knife, a blanket, and a knapsack with bread and salt pork in it—and a flask of brandy. Each man, of course, carried his musket, and every Ranger could hit the size of a dollar at a hundred yards.

Rogers' Rangers were the Special Forces, the Green Berets of the French and Indian War. They operated under these specific instructions from Major General Shirley:

> From time to time, to use your best endeavours to distress the French and allies by sacking, burning, and destroying their houses, barns, barracks, canoes, and battoes [bateaux], and by killing their cattle of every kind; and at all times to endeavour to way-lay, attack and destroy their convoys of provisions by land and water in any part of the country . . .

The British commanders had learned the value of fighting Indians as the Indians fought. The English regulars despised the provincials, but they felt differently about Captain Robert Rogers and his Rangers, whose exploits were soon as well known in England as in New England. The Indians had their ideas about Robert Rogers too. They called him the White Devil and tried to avoid argument with him and his men.

The original Ranger company was composed entirely of New Hampshire fighters led by Rogers. His second lieutenant was John Stark.

John Stark

John Stark was born in Londonderry, August 28, 1728. He grew up in Derryfield (Manchester) when the family moved there. Like Rogers, he took early to the wilderness and developed a strong physique through tramping, hunting, fishing, and exploring.

Stark went on a hunting trip along Bakers River in Rumney in April 1752 with his brother William, David Stinson, and Amos Eastman. Alone, Stark was surprised and captured by St. Francis Indians, who asked him which way the others had gone. He gave them the wrong direction, but unfortunately William and Eastman fired a signal to tell him where they were. When the Indians fired on them, Stark knocked up their guns. Stinson was killed, William Stark escaped, and John Stark and Amos Eastman were taken captive to St. Francis.

Stark was not an amenable captive. When the Indians forced him to run the gauntlet, he seized a club and used it on his tormentors. He refused to hoe corn, calling it women's work. Defiantly he cut down the corn and left the weeds, then threw his hoe into the river. Delighted by his boldness, the Indians called him the Young Chief. Stark spent several months among them, learning their ways and gaining a good knowledge of their language. He liked the St. Francis Indians, and they liked him. He always said he was well treated during his captivity and accounted the experience important in his life. Massachusetts commissioners, sent to Canada to ransom prisoners, redeemed Eastman for $60 but had to pay $103 for John Stark.

Stark quickly distinguished himself as Rogers' lieutenant. He was promoted to captain for gallantry in action after a notable exploit.

The Woods Fight

On January 15, 1757, Rogers with Stark, an ensign, and fifty Rangers left Fort Edward to reconnoiter. At Fort William Henry they picked up reinforcements, snowshoes, and provisions and started down Lake George on the ice, moving only a few miles a day. About halfway between Ticonderoga and Crown Point they came on a French supply convoy of ten sleds. Stark, with twenty men, took the lead sled. In all, the Ranger party captured three sleds with their stores, seven prisoners, and six horses. The rest of the convoy fled back to Ticonderoga, alerting a strong French force there.

Breaking one of their own rules—to come and go by different routes—the Rangers started back to Fort William Henry the way they had come, snowshoeing in single file. They were ambushed by a large body of French and Indians. Scattering, each man for himself in a desperate fight, the Rangers fired from behind trees, Stark covering their rear. Rogers was twice wounded, once in the head, in a fierce woods fight that raged all afternoon. Fourteen of his men were killed, six wounded, and six taken prisoner, but of the French and Indian force of 250 only 134 were alive to retreat at dark to Ticonderoga.

Taking the wounded and the French captives, John Stark then began a long all-night journey through the snow and bitter cold. When they reached the shore of Lake George the next morning, he and two other Rangers volunteered to make a forced march of forty miles to Fort William Henry. They reached it, exhausted, that night, and a fresh party was sent out with hand sleds to bring back the wounded.

Lord Jeffery Amherst

Brought up as a page in the household of the Duke of Dorset, Jeffery Amherst entered the army as an aide-de-camp to General John Ligonier in the War of the Austrian Succession. He was made a lieutenant colonel in 1745, saw more active service on the Continent, and returned to England. He was made colonel of the 15th Regiment of Foot before he was sent back for further continental duty.

In January 1758, Amherst was ordered back to England and commissioned a major general. Then he was dispatched to America with fourteen thousand men to retake Louisburg. Shelling the citadel until the town and fortress were in ruins, Amherst took Louisburg with a combined land and sea attack after a siege of two months. More than five thousand French surrendered, and Amherst took eleven French battleships, forty heavy guns, thousands of stands of small arms, and a great quantity of stores.

Succeeding a number of less effective general officers, Amherst was made commander in chief of all the British forces in America and went on to capture the French strongholds of Ticonderoga and Crown Point in 1758.

Rogers and his New Hampshire men were also involved in this battle, and so magnificently did they perform that, at age twenty-six, Rogers was promoted to major, ordered to train more Rangers, and placed in command of nine Ranger companies. The Rangers were then made part of the British regular army, and Rogers and his officers, John Stark among them, were given king's commissions to replace their New Hampshire rank.

Four Ranger companies under Rogers were with Lord Loudoun when he sailed for Halifax with six thousand men. There he was joined by five thousand British regulars and a naval force, but to Rogers' disgust, Loudoun returned to New York without striking a blow.

Obliteration of St. Francis

The Rangers had already served under Amherst at Ticonderoga and at Crown Point. Then, on September 13, 1758, General Amherst ordered Rogers and his men against St. Francis. For a hundred years the Abnakis of this village had murdered, pillaged, and, despite previous raids on them, been the scourge of New England. Amherst's order read:

> You are this night to set out with the detachment, as ordered yesterday, viz., of 200 men, which you will take under your command and proceed to Missiquoi Bay, from whence you will march and attack the enemy on the south side of the river St. Lawrence in such manner as you shall judge most effectual to disgrace the enemy, and for the success and honour of his majesty's arms.
>
> Take your revenge, but don't forget that tho' these villains had dastardly and promiscuously murdered the women and children of all ages, it is my orders that no women or children are killed or hurt.

Ten days later the Rangers reached St. Francis undetected. The Indians had held a dance and celebration and were sleeping heavily. Half an hour before sunrise the Rangers fell on them from all sides, and before the St. Francis warriors could reach their guns, they were dead. A few who attempted to escape down the Kennebec were shot in their canoes.

Daylight showed six hundred scalps, most of them English, dangling on poles in front of the doors of the huts. The enraged Rangers fired every house, except those containing supplies. Those they confiscated. By noon of September 24 the village of St. Francis had been wiped out.

End of the French and Indian War

In 1759 General James Wolfe, second in command to Amherst, with five thousand men scaled the heights of Quebec to the Plains of Abraham and took the city, though both he and the French commander, Louis Joseph Montcalm de Saint-Veran, were mortally wounded in the battle. Six hundred Rangers and seventy Indians formed the advance guard of the English when Amherst moved against Montreal. The French surrendered, and the British troops entered the city on September 8, 1760. The war was over, and France was expelled from Canada. The depredations of the French and their Indians on New England were finally ended. The Peace of Paris was signed in 1763.

Aftermath

The conqueror of Canada, tall, lean, and formal Lord Jeffery Amherst, was made governor of Virginia in recognition of his services, but he resigned when King George III decided that as governor he should live there. Made a Knight of the Bath, Amherst was given twenty thousand acres in New York and in 1770 was made governor of the Isle of Guernsey. During the Revolution he commanded all the British forces in England and in 1796 attained the rank of field marshal, highest in the royal army. Towns in New Hampshire, Massachusetts, and Virginia are all named for him, and he is celebrated in song as "a soldier of the king."

Rogers and his Rangers were not yet finished when the war ended. With two hundred Rangers, Rogers was sent to effect the surrender of the French forts to the west. They pushed as far as Detroit, taking over French outposts as they went.

When he came home in 1761, Robert Rogers married Elizabeth Browne, daughter of the Reverend Arthur Browne of Portsmouth, which Rogers considered his home. For his services in the French and Indian War he was given four or five hundred acres of land at Rumford and later three thousand acres in what became southern Vermont. In 1762 Rogers gave his father-in-law much of his land at Rumford, together with a family of three Negroes and a thirteen-year-old Indian boy.

After being lionized in London, Rogers was made commandant of the fort at Michilimackinac. His wife stayed there in the wilderness with him for two years, and they had one child; but Rogers, though he may have tried, was not a good husband and could not find peace without a war. He became involved in questionable land deals, in drunken brawls, and in other unsavory schemes and activities. Finally he was arrested on charges of conspiring with the French, but the charge was dismissed for lack of evidence.

Rogers fought against the Cherokee in South Carolina, captained a New York company in the defense of Detroit against Pontiac, served as an adventurer under the Dey of Algiers, and landed in debtors' prison in London. His brother freed him by assuming his debts. In 1778 the New Hampshire Assembly approved the petition of Elizabeth Browne Rogers for a divorce.

John Stark, so durable that he was never once wounded in any action, was made of sterner and more sober stuff. On August 20, 1758, he married Elizabeth Page, daughter of Captain Caleb Page. Like Robert Rogers, John and William Stark, were still British army officers, though on inactive duty and on half pay. John Stark settled a new township near Londonderry, which was at first called Starktown, then Dumbarton, and devoted himself to his extensive farm and mills.

There were other Rangers who, like Rogers, found adjustment to peace difficult. One was Lieutenant William Phillips of Rumford. Phillips, who was part Indian, had himself been caught by the Indians and tied to a tree to await disposal, but escaped. On their way home from St. Francis he and several others lived on bark and tree buds. They were about to kill and eat an Indian boy when, fortunately for the boy, they caught a muskrat and ate it instead. Phillips later got married in a Rumford tavern, but his wife left him to join the Shaker colony at Canterbury. After that Phillips lived by hunting, fishing, and (so Douton says, italicizing the word) *stealing*.

CHAPTER NINE

The Wentworth Dynasty

The Wentworth name was old and distinguished in England long before it stamped itself on the history and geography of New Hampshire.

There were many branches of the family, all descended from a William Wentworth who was born in Yorkshire and died in 1308. A Baron Wentworth signed the letter to the Pope recommending the divorce of Henry VIII and Catharine of Aragon. Thomas Wentworth was the first Earl of Cleveland. Peter Wentworth, a Puritan leader in Parliament, was imprisoned in the Tower of London and died there. His grandson, Sir Peter Wentworth, although he was a Cromwellian, refused to serve as a commissioner in the trial of Charles I. Charles Wentworth was the Marquis of Rockingham and William Wentworth the Earl of Strafford. The Wentworths were influential men in England with great estates and widespread family connections, which were very useful to their descendants and relatives in New Hampshire.

William Wentworth, a cousin of the chancellor of Charles I, was the first of the name in New Hampshire. He was one of the signers of the Exeter Combination, although it was at Dover that as an octogenarian he distinguished himself in the Indian raid of 1689.

When New Hampshire was part of Massachusetts Bay, the governor resided in Boston and ruled from a distance. Actual authority in New Hampshire was vested in the lieutenant governor, who ruled from Portsmouth with an appointed Council and an elected General Assembly.

 John Wentworth, son of William, became lieutenant governor of

New Hampshire as a replacement for George Vaughan, who was dismissed by Governor Samuel Shute of Massachusetts Bay after a quarrel.

Wentworth received his royal commission (countersigned by Joseph Addison, who was then England's secretary of state) early in December 1717. This was the beginning of the long reign of the Wentworths and their kin and connections–the Atkinsons, Vaughans, Livermores, Rindges, and others of Portsmouth's interrelated mercantile aristocracy –which would last until the Revolution.

Born June 16, 1672, John Wentworth had been a sea captain in early life, but, like the rest of the Wentworths, he became a merchant and, again like them, highly successful. Belknap says, "He was a gentleman of good natural abilities, much improved by conversation; remarkably civil and kind to strangers; respectful to the ministers of the gospel; a lover of good men of all denominations; compassionate and bountiful to the poor, courteous and affable to all."

John Wentworth was also an experienced politician and popular with the people. He had served for five years in the New Hampshire Council, been appointed councillor to Queen Anne from 1711 to 1712, and made a justice of the peace, serving from 1715 to 1718. Lieutenant Governor Wentworth did his best to develop the province of New Hampshire. He sought markets for its masts, tar, pitch, and turpentine. He encouraged the mining of iron ore on what was called the Two-Mile Strip near Dover.

Annoyed at the continued encroachments of Massachusetts Bay on New Hampshire territory, this Wentworth tried to preempt its grant of Rumford to Massachusetts families. He failed, but he succeeded in provoking the ire of Governor Jonathan Belcher.

Jonathan Belcher

Belcher was the brother-in-law of George Vaughan, whom John Wentworth had replaced–a bad beginning. He was also married to Mary Partridge, daughter of an earlier lieutenant governor of New Hampshire, and that did not help either. Belcher, who had traveled in

Europe for some years after his graduation from Harvard, was, as his father had been, a prosperous merchant. He was also in the right place at the right time. He was in England when Shute's successor, Governor William Burnet, died, made it clear that he was available, and was appointed royal governor of both Massachusetts Bay and New Hampshire in January 1730.

Belcher quickly demonstrated his dislike of John Wentworth by taking away some of his prerogatives and cutting his income as lieutenant governor. After that he dismissed or curtailed the authority of some of Wentworth's principal appointees. They did not like that at all.

Then as now, politicians had ways of expressing their resentment. Theodore Atkinson was married to one of John Wentworth's daughters. He held posts as naval officer, sheriff of New Hampshire, and collector of customs. Belcher stripped Atkinson of his naval rank, removed him from the customs office, and made one of his own henchmen joint sheriff. When Governor Belcher, soon after he was appointed, ordered a troop of horse to escort him into Portsmouth, Atkinson arrived late, carrying only half his staff of office as sheriff. Reprimanded by Belcher for his tardiness, Atkinson explained that, being only half a sheriff, he had only half a horse to ride.

Lieutenant Governor John Wentworth died in 1730. Governor Belcher—irascible, domineering, but sycophantic with his superiors in England—was victimized by his political enemies in 1741 and dismissed.

Benning Wentworth

Immediately on Belcher's dismissal, Benning Wentworth, eldest of John Wentworth's sixteen children, and his brother-in-law, Theodore Atkinson, began to work for the separation of Massachusetts Bay and New Hampshire. They had powerful friends at the English court, and they exerted all their efforts. They won, and in 1741 Benning Wentworth was made the first royal governor of New Hampshire.

This Wentworth had been born in Portsmouth in 1696. He graduated fifth in his class from Harvard. This does not mean that he was a fine scholar. It means that even in patrician Boston and Cambridge the Wentworths were recognized as wealthy aristocrats, for rank at Harvard graduations was granted in accordance with the social standing of the student's family.

Benning Wentworth went into the family business and married Abigail Rock, daughter of another prominent merchant. He made many trips to England and became a member first of the Assembly, then of the Council.

The man who would be governor of New Hampshire for the almost incredible term of twenty-five years was personable, dignified, and capable. He could be charming, and he was certainly ambitious. A leader in the Church of England and the social hierarchy of Portsmouth, he strongly upheld the royal authority in New Hampshire. In a sense, he realized the dream of John Mason, for Benning Wentworth lived like

A colonial gentleman dressed in the fashion of the mid-eighteenth century.

George The Third by the Grace of God of Great Britain France & Ireland King [illegible]

To All to whom these Presents shall come Greeting **Whereas** Our Loyal Subjects inhabiting a [illegible] act of Land within Our Province of New Hampshire by the Name of New Durham — have humbly petitioned & requested Us, that they may be Erected & Incorporated into a Township & infranchised with the same Powers & Priviledges with other Towns within Our said Province & which they by Law have and Enjoy And it appearing to Us to be Conducive to the General Good of Our said Province as well as to the said Inhabitants in particular, by maintaining good Order & Encouraging the Culture of the Lands, that the same should be done, Know Ye therefore That We of our Especial Grace certain Knowledge, and for the Encouragement and Promotion of the good End and purposes aforesaid by and with the Advice of Our Trusty and Well Beloved **Benning Wentworth** Esqr Our Governor and Commander in Chief [illegible] and of Our Council for said Province of New Hampshire Have Erected and Ordained, And by these Presents for Us Our Heirs & Successors Do Will and Ordain that Our loving Subjects residing on the Tract of Land aforesaid or that shall hereafter reside & improve thereon the same being limited & bounded as follows — Beginning at the South Westerly Corner of a Tract of Land granted unto Ebenezer Varney W.m Wentworth & others upon & at Rochester head Line & from thence running Westerly by said head Line five Miles, & to continue the breadth of five miles extending from the said head Line so far Northwardly as to make a Tract of Land Equal to Six Miles square, adjoining to the said Tract of Land granted to the said Ebenezer Varney & W.m Wentworth and others and the Head line of the said Tract of Land hereby granted to be a Parralel Line with the head Line of Rochester and the said Lines to be parralel with Each other shall be And by these presents are declared, and Ordained to be a Town Corporate, and are hereby Erected & incorporated into a Body Politic and Corporate to have a Continuance untill, His Majesty's pleasure shall be Signified to the Contrary by the name of New Durham with all the Powers Authorities priviledges Immunities and Franchises which any other Town in said Province by Law hold and Enjoy always reserving to Us Our heirs and Successors All white Pine Trees that are or shall be found growing & being on the said Tract of Land fit for the Use of Our Royal Navy, reserving to Us Our Heirs and Successors the Power & Right of dividing said Town when it shall appear necessary & convenient for the benefit of the Inhabitants thereof Provided Neverthelefs And it is hereby declared that this Our Charter & Grant is not intended or shall in any manner be Construed to Extend to or Affect the private Property of the Soil within the Limits aforesaid And as the several Towns within Our said Province of New Hampshire are by the Laws thereof Enabled & authorized to assemble & by the Majority of the Votes present to Chuse all such Officers & transact such Affairs as by the said Laws are declared, We do by these presents nominate and appoint Major Thomas Tash — to Call the first Meeting [illegible] any time within Twenty days from the date hereof giving Legal Notice of the time & design of holding such Meeting after which the Annual Meeting of said Town for the Choice of such Officers & management of the Affairs aforesaid shall be held within the same on the first Monday in March.

In Testimony whereof We have caused the Seal of Our said Province to be hereunto affixed Witnefs Benning Wentworth Esqr Our Governor and Commander in Chief in and over Our said Province of New Hampshire the Seventh day of December in the Third Year of Our Reign Annoque Domini 1762.

[illegible]

Patent for a grant of land within the province of New Hampshire by George III.

an English nobleman, amassed vast estates, and acted as befitted a king's landed servant, who was just a little farther removed from the court than his fellows at home.

Quickly after Benning Wentworth's accession the long-standing boundary dispute with Massachusetts Bay was settled, and much in New Hampshire's favor. Among other things the province gained the town of Rumford (Concord), which John Wentworth had lost.

In the Indian wars, Governor Wentworth backed his New Hampshire men with money and supplies and supported William Vaughan's plan for the capture of Louisburg in 1745. Many times he was thanked by New Hampshire military leaders for his marked attention to the troops. Wentworth also had disputes with the Assembly which, he claimed, usurped some of his powers in the appointing of chaplains, surgeons, and commissaries, and in selecting committees to handle various public matters—matters in which patronage money was involved.

Benning Wentworth did well for his farmers, fishermen, lumbermen, and tradesmen, and New Hampshire grew steadily in wealth and power under his rule. The royal governor also did very well for himself.

He granted new townships by the score. Some lands went to veterans of the various Indian wars for their services, but more went to wealthy men in Massachusetts, because they were the highest bidders for land on which they expected to realize handsome profits. These investors paid high fees to Wentworth for the grants and in each new township reserved five hundred acres, free and unencumbered, for the royal governor.

Three lines of townships were laid out on both sides of the Connecticut River for sixty miles. New York claimed the land on the west side, which eventually became Vermont, but so did New Hampshire. In the one year of 1761, Benning Wentworth made eighteen grants of land east of the Connecticut and sixty west. In total he made 138 grants west of the Connecticut, each time obtaining fees, presents, and his five hundred acres. One township that would become famous in New Hampshire history he named for himself, Bennington.

Benning Wentworth realized another of Captain John Mason's dreams. He built a manor house, a rambling mansion, which was completed in 1750. Large, ornate, with castlelike gates and many wings, the Wentworth mansion—which eventually had over forty rooms—looked out to sea at Little Harbour. Outside, it had outbuildings, offices, and stabling for thirty horses. Inside, it had stately reception rooms, smaller parlors, and many guest rooms. With its English china, silver, and furniture, it was a fit place for entertaining Lord Loudoun, Sir William Pepperell, Governor William Shirley, George Whitefield, and the other greats of the colonies. Inevitably, George Washington was a guest in later years.

Sabatis and Plausawa

New Hampshire was tense during the Indians wars. Portsmouth's taverns were crowded and noisy as men went off to fight. Occasionally there were disturbances, and there was an outbreak of mob violence in 1754.

Two Indians, Sabatis and Plausawa, ventured into Canterbury in 1753, even though Sabatis was known to have taken part in the abduction of two men there the year before. According to Sylvester, they spent the night drinking with Peter Bowen and his friend Morril. In the morning the Indians asked Bowen to carry their baggage to their canoe on his horse. Bowen agreed, but took the precaution of unloading their guns without their knowing it. On the way to the canoe, as Bowen later told it, first one Indian, then the other, drew on him. Bowen struck a tomahawk into Sabatis' skull and then, knowing he would not be safe with the other Indian at large, dispatched Plausawa in the same way. What part Morril took in the transaction is unknown.

Both Bowen and Morril were indicted for murder and taken to Portsmouth for trail. The night before the trail was scheduled, a mob of men armed with axes and crowbars broke into the jail and freed the prisoners. Rewards were offered for the recapture of the two men and for the arrest and conviction of the rioters, but they were never claimed, nor was the matter pressed. Feeling against Indians ran so high that both the slaying and the act of the rioters won public approval.

New Settlements

When the French and Indian War finally came to a victorious close, taxes to defray its cost were high. Goods were scarce. Men had been killed and families burned out. Times were hard, but the relief from fear of further attacks was such that New Hampshire, which had been particularly hard hit during the long years of struggle, was jubilant. The French had been soundly defeated and an end put to the Indian depredations from Canada. Without the guns, ammunition, and supplies zealously provided by the French, the Indians were helpless. They could no longer dispute the advance of New England settlers into what had been their home and their hunting and fishing grounds. The Indians withdrew, and after nearly a century of cruel conflict there was lasting peace.

Families moved out of the garrisons back into their homes. Men were free to fell trees, burn the stumps, clear the fields, and plant seeds in the rich forest earth. In the port towns commerce, which had been at a standstill, began again. New people came into New Hampshire. Its population, which had been held down by the wars, mounted rapidly.

The house built in 1734 by the Reverend Timothy Walker, who lived in it until his death in 1782.

Soldiers who had seen the country while on active service and knew its worth were eager to claim the lands awarded them as bounty. Speculators sought new land ventures. Settlers poured up the Connecticut River valley from Connecticut and Massachusetts.

The White Mountain region had been known ever since the exploration of Captain Neale and Darby Field in 1632, and passes through the mountains were in use; but possession by the Indians had made settlement impossible. In the southwest corner of the province Keene had been founded by settlers from Massachusetts in 1733, and its meetinghouse had been built two years later; but the Indians had made it impossible to hold the town. They attacked it in 1745, and in 1746 burned the town while its people defended themselves from behind the walls of the fort. The town had to be abandoned in 1747. It was occupied again in 1753 but suffered another Indian attack in 1755. Now Keene and the other townships in the west could get on with the business of living again.

New settlers penetrated farther north. They built log cabins, stuffing the crevices with moss or clay, and roofed them with bark or split boards. Windows had no glass and were usually closed with shutters. Fires against the cold in winter and the mosquitoes in summer sent their smoke out through holes in the roof. Smoke was used to protect the cattle, too, from mosquitoes and black flies. Cooking was done over an open-hearth fire and baking in ovens built outside the house. As soon as the people had sawmills to provide boards and blacksmiths to make

The Governor Benning Wentworth House, *c.* 1750, facing Little Harbor.

nails, they built more substantial houses, luxurious compared to these first primitive quarters.

Growth was slower as the stream of immigration reached the beautiful, but cold and harsh, White Mountains. Jackson on Carter Notch, where the Wildcat River roars and tumbles down the mountainside, was not settled until 1778, though the spot had been known for a century. For twelve years Benjamin Copp and his family were the only inhabitants. Five new families joined them in 1790. One of the new men was Joseph Pinkham, for whom famed Pinkham Notch is named. It is said that the Pinkhams brought all their worldly goods on a sled drawn over the snow by a trained pig.

Preventive Medicine

In whatever direction New Hampshire expanded, Benning Wentworth profited. In less than twenty years he acquired some hundred thousand acres of new land. Population climbed to about 52,000. Shipping and trading flourished, but, as always, with growth came new dangers.

Because of its constant traffic with foreign countries and with the larger seaport of Boston, there were frequent outbreaks of smallpox. To prevent infection and contagion Portsmouth built a hospital on a small island in the river below the town. Called the Pest House, it was used to quarantine those who had already contracted the disease. In 1764, with the smallpox rampant again, Portsmouth went in for preventive measures. Its selectmen had a fence built across the road at Great Swamp and a small house put up. In it all travelers who came from Boston by land were disinfected along with their baggage. Only when they had been thoroughly smoked did the guards issue certificates permitting them to pass into the town. Travelers coming from Boston by water received the same treatment when they disembarked.

Charges Against Benning Wentworth

There was a maidservant in the Wentworth mansion named Martha Hilton. Descended from a family important in the founding of New Hampshire, she was a beautiful young woman of clear intelligence and sharp wit. When reprimanded by an older woman for the boldness of her dress, she said spiritedly, "Never mind how I look; I yet shall ride in my own chariot, ma'am." She proved a good prophet.

Benning Wentworth's wife had died. On his sixtieth birthday, to the consternation of his family and the joy of the gossips, the royal governor of New Hampshire married his maid. This frivolity on the part of a dignified governor, who dressed in the height of fashion, even to a blond peruke falling over his shoulders, was one of the criticisms leveled against him in 1766 by a Peter Livius, who had political ambitions of his own. Livius' chief complaint to London was that Wentworth was enriching himself through unrestricted land grants and neglecting the other duties of his office. Fortunately for Benning Wentworth, who had governed New Hampshire well for a quarter century, he had a capable defender on the scene in London.

Sir John Wentworth

John, son of Mark Hunking Wentworth, wealthy merchant and extensive landowner, and of Elizabeth Rindge Wentworth, was Benning Wentworth's nephew. He had graduated from Harvard in 1755—in the same class as Samuel Adams of Massachusetts Bay—and then spent

John Wentworth

Frances Wentworth

much of his time in England effectively looking after the Wentworth interests there. Intelligent and charming, this John Wentworth was a favorite with such influential noblemen as Lords Rockingham, Hillsborough, and Strafford. In 1763 Wentworth was appointed one of the agents for New Hampshire, and he helped obtain repeal of the much-hated Stamp Act.

John Wentworth had little trouble disproving the charges made against his uncle, who was quickly vindicated by the Privy Council. Peter Livius was placated with a government post in Canada, and Benning Wentworth was exonerated.

Nevertheless, Benning Wentworth's tenure had been long, and it seemed time for a change. To the colonial authorities in England it was quite apparent who the new governor should be. On August 11, 1767, when he was not quite thirty years old, John Wentworth was commissioned royal governor of New Hampshire. At the same time he was made surveyor of the King's woods for all the American colonies.

New Hampshire's new governor sailed from England in the spring of 1767. Landing in Charleston, South Carolina, he traveled north at his leisure, welcomed everywhere as surveyor, and visiting prominent people on his way home. Already popular as his uncle's nephew and for his work in the Stamp Act repeal, he was acclaimed in Portsmouth when he arrived. There were elaborate ceremonies when he took the oath of office on June 13, 1767. A cavalcade of ladies and gentlemen formed a procession in his honor, a proclamation of his royal appointments was read, and regiments of foot and infantry paraded. Nathaniel Adams, the annalist of Portsmouth, reported that after a full day of celebration, "The Governor, Council, and gentlemen present, partook of an elegant entertainment prepared for the occasion."

The reign of John Wentworth began auspiciously. The wars were over; prosperity had returned. In contrast to relations between belligerent Massachusetts Bay and the parent country, those between New Hampshire and England were friendly. Its people were loyal and happy under Britain's rule. Through his wise and generous administration, the young governor enhanced his popularity, and there was a genuine affection for King George III in the province.

In the first year of his governorship, about two weeks after the death of her husband, Wentworth married Frances (Deering) Atkinson, widow of his cousin and Harvard classmate Theodore Atkinson, Jr. Frances Wentworth became the admired hostess of the family mansion.

As his uncle had done, John Wentworth granted new townships in New Hampshire, receiving the same profits and the same reservations of land. One new town, founded in 1762, he named Francestown for his wife; another, also for her, he named Deering. A new town at the foot of Lake Winnipesaukee he named Wolfeborough for the conqueror of Quebec. Wentworth divided New Hampshire into counties and named three of them for his English friends and patrons: Rockingham, Strafford, and Hillsborough.

New Hampshire thrived under John Wentworth, who built much-needed roads into the interior of the province and who supported education, not only through his office but also by his own generosity.

Dartmouth College

The idea for a school for Indians came from John Sergeant, missionary at Stockbridge in Massachusetts Bay. The school was founded toward the end of 1754 by Dr. Eleazar Wheelock in Lebanon, Con-

William Legge, Earl of Dartmouth

necticut. Because Colonel Joshua Moor had given the land, a house, and a schoolhouse for the project, it became known as Moor's (or More's) Charity School. As the area around Labanon became crowded, a new site was sought for the school, which now admitted a number of white students to be educated along with the Indians in agriculture and literary subjects.

Funds were raised in the colonies, and an Indian preacher, Samson Occum, who had been a student at the school, raised £10,000 for it in England and Scotland. This money was put at the disposal of a board of trustees headed by the Earl of Dartmouth.

Various localities competed for the school, but Dr. Wheelock and the trustees in England chose Hanover, New Hampshire, on the east bank of the Connecticut River. Governor Wentworth granted the charter. Benning Wentworth gave five hundred acres for its site, and

Drawing of the inaugural ceremonies at Dartmouth College in 1769.
A front view of Dartmouth College, with the chapel and hall.

other large grants of land were made to the new institution, to be known as Dartmouth College. Wheelock was declared founder and first president, and the New Hampshire Assembly voted him £100 to cover his expenses in moving from Lebanon to Hanover.

Originally a trade school for Indians, Dartmouth College opened in 1770 as a "seminary of literature." It had twenty-eight students, eighteen of them white, the rest Indians. In 1771 Dartmouth had four graduates, one of them John Wheelock, son of the president. At first the college consisted of a few huts made of green logs on its campus. Dartmouth Hall, closely resembling Nassau Hall at Princeton, was completed in 1791. John Wentworth, who served on the board of trustees, gave generously to the school and influenced others to give.

John Phillips, founder of the Phillips Exeter Academy.

Two fine examples of New Hampshire colonial architecture. *Right:* The Captain John Clark House, *c.* 1750. This central-chimney house is typical of many Portsmouth dwellings of the era. Triangular pediments over door and windows accent the simple exterior. *Bottom:* The Chase House at Strawbery Banke was built in 1762. With its fine doorway and other elegant features, it was one of the finest dwellings in its neighborhood when it was first built.

He even gave each of its first four graduates land for farms. Franklin B. Sanborn says flatly that Governor John Wentworth had more to do with the founding of Dartmouth College than Eleazar Wheelock.

Phillips Exeter Academy

Phillips Academy, the first chartered academy in America, was founded in Andover, Massachusetts, by Samuel and John Phillips in 1788. In 1781 John Phillips, preacher and judge, gave gifts totaling $63,000 to establish the companion Phillips Academy in Exeter, New Hampshire. As stated in the deed of gift, the purpose of Phillips Exeter was "the promoting of Piety and Virtue, and for the education of youth in the English, Latin, and Greek languages, in Writing, Arithmetic, Music, and the Art of Speaking, Practical Geometry, Logic, and Geography, and such other of the Liberal Arts and Sciences or languages as opportunity may hereinafter permit."

Made principal of the new academy in the same year that he graduated from Harvard, Benjamin Abbot, who taught most of the Latin, Greek, and mathematics himself, established Exeter's high standing and repute. The school gained the George Washington seal of approval when Washington sent two of his nephews there. In New Hampshire, Daniel Webster is perhaps the most famous of Exeter's many famous graduates.

Wolfeborough (now Wolfeboro)

One of the roads that Governor John Wentworth had built was the 45-mile route from Portsmouth to Wolfeborough. Cut through rough country, the road was so bad that the governor's lady complained about it with a mixture of vexation and amusement; but it was a road, and it went somewhere. As early as 1768 Wentworth began to build a great country estate in Wolfeborough. It became one of the finest north of Maryland. It was not quite as large but it was thought to have been better built, equipped, and maintained than was Washington's Mount Vernon at the time.

Wentworth had nearly 6,000 acres at Wolfeborough. His park measured about 600 fenced acres; his house, built by good workmen, was

102 feet long by 41 feet wide. There were two stables and two coach houses, each 106 by 40 feet. One barn, "framed, boarded, and painted completely," was 106 feet long, 40 feet wide, and 18 to 22 feet high. This magnificent estate had its own carpenter, blacksmith, and cabinet-making shops. John Wentworth put the value of the whole at £22,000 sterling—the same amount of money that Captain John Mason had expended in founding New Hampshire.

Governor Wentworth's estate and the road he built to reach it led to more migrations into the lake region of New Hampshire.

Last Years as a Province

The population of New Hampshire increased 40 percent during the administration of Governor John Wentworth, rising from 52,000 when he took office and continuing to rise after he left it, so that it was 141,885 by 1790.

Newspapers were established. The first was the *New-Hampshire Gazette and Historical Chronicle*, which was published in Portsmouth by Daniel Fowle. This was New Hampshire's conservative and loyalist newspaper. Eight years later an opposition sheet, Whig and independent, *The New-Hampshire Mercury and Weekly Advertiser*, began publishing in Portsmouth.

Transport improved. In 1761, while Benning Wentworth was still governor, an Englishman named John Stavers began to run a stage, a curricle drawn by two horses, from Portsmouth to Boston. It made the round trip once a week. This vehicle was supplanted in 1763 by the "Portsmouth Flying Stage Coach," drawn by four horses or, when snow or mud made it necessary, by six. Stavers opened the Earl of Halifax Inn, a large wooden hotel of three stories, in Portsmouth in 1770, and the Portsmouth Flyer ran to and from this inn.

By 1773 New Hampshire, which had had only four towns when it first became a royal province, had 147 towns.

CHAPTER TEN

The Revolution

Preoccupied with its national and commercial interests in Europe and other parts of the world, and with the wars it fought to obtain and protect them, Great Britain had allowed its American colonies to go much their own way. There were laws governing trading and shipping, imports and exports; but they were generally and cheerfully evaded in the colonies, and England did little to enforce them. In the early 1760's she decided to tighten and strengthen her government of the colonies, which were growing in population and in wealth and, England noted with annoyance, flouting her regulations and working against her interests if they interfered with their own.

The war with France had been expensive, and England was determined that the colonies, which had benefited largely from its successful conclusion, bear part of the expense. It rankled that Massachusetts Bay had continued to trade profitably with the enemy while the war was in progress and had profiteered piratically in selling provisions and supplies to the British forces. To correct, and in some measure to punish Massachusetts, England passed and began stringent enforcement of restrictive laws.

The Sugar Act and Writs of Assistance

In 1761 William Pitt, England's great Whig prime minister, ordered the Royal Navy to stamp out smuggling in America. This was taken as a mortal affront in Boston and other colonial ports, where smuggling was a long-established way of life. To help enforce customs regulations and collect fees, colonial courts were ordered to issue writs of assistance. Under these general search warrants, customs officers were empowered to search and seize in any suspect quarter. Opposition to them was headed by James Otis, who made a four-hour speech against the writs before Governor Thomas Hutchinson of Massachusetts Bay. Otis' assistants coined the Revolutionary slogan "Taxation Without Representation."

John Hancock himself, wealthiest of the wealthy Boston merchants, was indicted for smuggling wines, and his ship *Liberty* was seized. Hancock had a good lawyer, John Adams, so the suit was dropped, but he never got the *Liberty* back. The British used her as a coast guard vessel until a Newport, Rhode Island, mob burned her.

In defiance of trade laws, the colonies, rather than buy sugar and molasses from British sources in the Caribbean, had been getting them from the French for 25 to 40 percent less. A sugar act of 1764 cut the British duty on molasses, but a duty continued to be collected. Additional duties were placed on sugar, coffee, wines, silks, indigo, and other frequently imported articles.

The Stamp Act

As a port colony New Hampshire suffered under the new restrictions, but managed either to evade or to endure them. She acted differently when England passed the Stamp Act in 1765. Intended to raise revenue for the crown, this act required that a stamp, ranging in cost from a halfpenny for a newspaper or pamphlet up to ten pounds on licenses and contracts, be placed on all papers and legal documents. The protest against the Stamp Act was immediate and violent. Newspapers and Whig politicians denounced it.

Like newspapers in the other colonies, the *New-Hampshire Gazette* for October 31, 1765, appeared with a black mourning border around its pages. It denounced the Stamp Act bitterly. Yet there was hardly need. Governor Benning Wentworth found that he had received no official notice of the act. That seemed to be a valid excuse for not trying to enforce a measure that he saw was much against the popular will.

George Messerve, who was in England at the time, was appointed distributor of the stamps for New Hampshire. Learning of the opposition to the stamps, he resigned as soon as he landed in Boston. When he reached home in Portsmouth, he resigned all over again. Portsmouth, which had made preparations to hang him in effigy, applauded him instead. As there was thus no agent to receive them, the stamps sent to Boston for New Hampshire were simply stored away. They never reached New Hampshire.

There was a near riot anyway. November 5 was the anniversary of the Gunpowder Plot, Guy Fawkes' unsuccessful plan to blow up the British Houses of Parliament. This holiday had always been an occasion for bonfires and celebration, and there seemed to be an added excuse for riot now. The magistrates put extra guards on the streets, but they were not needed. The country people marched on Portsmouth to protest, but they turned around and went home when told that the stamps were not going to be used. The next day in Portsmouth bells tolled, and a funeral procession was held for the Goddess of Liberty. She was put into her grave, then quickly resurrected, signs of life being detected when it was known that New Hampshire had rejected the stamps.

In part, the repeal of the Stamp Act was the work of John Wentworth. Other opponents of the act, in Parliament, had referred to Americans as "Sons of Liberty." The phrase caught on and was adopted by the most belligerent of those who clamored for independence from Great Britain. The Sons of Liberty became the name of their secret society, which was active by 1766.

Revolutionary Versus Loyalist Sentiment

The American Revolution was in no sense the concerted uprising of an abused people against implacable tyranny. It did not come on suddenly or unaided. It came on gradually over a long period of time, though its outbreak was provoked by a series of costly errors in judgment on the part of Britain and the fervor of propagandists in some of the colonies, particularly Massachusetts Bay. Boston had been resentful ever since the colony lost its original charter, and by this time Massachusetts had become a commercial rival of England.

In England the controversy over treatment of the colonies was political, the Whig party against the Tory party. Roughly, the Whigs were the liberals, and they were, generally, in favor of lenient treatment for the American colonies. The aristocratic Tories were the conservatives. They stood for tradition and for strict adherence to the rights of the English crown.

In the colonies the revolution was a social as well as a political conflict. It was a struggle of the common man, led by demagogues, against the crown officials and their staffs, the people who were in power or thrived under the government of England. Those who had much to lose, officials with crown appointments, merchants with profitable business connections in England, Anglican clergymen, and Congregational or Presbyterian ministers with ties to English or Scottish churches, were on the defensive against those who had little or nothing to lose and much that they wished hotly to gain. Personal and political animosities and class resentments motivated many of the leading aggressors. None of these distinctions were absolute. There were ministers and lawyers, laborers, farmers, and craftsmen on both sides.

There were also physical and temporal considerations. New England was an ocean away, and now generations removed, from England. Though they spoke its language and their antecedents were English, by the 1760's many in America knew England only as a possessive European power, almost as foreign as France or Spain.

Sentiment differed in town and country, in small and large towns. In farming communities, the ministers as well as the squires and the farmers were generally Whig, independent in spirit and by conviction. The port towns, which like Boston and Portsmouth were in continual communication with England through trade, were sharply divided. Lawyers, merchants, and physicians who had studied in England were mostly Tories, while their fellows were not. Led by the rabble-rousing Samuel Adams, the "Boston Mob," as it was called, was violently insistent upon separation from England.

Powerful in itself, Massachusetts Bay had, in one way or another, founded both Rhode Island and Connecticut. Twice it had controlled New Hampshire. Because its sentiments spread quickly to those colonies, Boston was the target of more restrictive acts. They, in turn, led to the attempted murder of Governor Hutchinson and the looting of

Advertiſement.

THIS is to give Notice to all ſuch Officers and Soldiers of the firſt, ſecond, and third New-Hampſhire Regiments, whoſe Furloughs are expired; thoſe who at different Times have been left ſick, and alſo to thoſe who were captured by the Enemy, and have been ſince retaken, or by any other Means made their eſcape, that they are required forthwith to join their Regiments at Head-Quarters. AND WHEREAS, there are numbers of Soldiers that have deſerted from ſaid Regiments, and many that have never yet joined them, now ſculking about the Country, probably willing to return to their Duty, but deterred from it through fear of Puniſhment: I DO, by conſent of his Excellency General WASHINGTON hereby promiſe them a full and free Pardon on condition they join their Regiments, or deliver themſelves up to ſome Officer of the Continental Army, on or before the twentieth Day of next March; but ſhould any one be ſo loſt to a ſenſe of his Duty, as to neglect this Opportunity, he muſt, if found, expect to ſuffer the ſeverities of the Martial Law, in that Caſe made and provided.

ENOCH POOR, Brigadier-General.

Valley-Forge-Camp, Pennſylvania, January 21ſt, 1778.

STATE OF NEW-HAMPSHIRE, February 17th, 1778.

THESE are to give Notice, that the Town of EXETER in this State, is appointed as a place of Rendezvous for the Soldiers deſcribed in the above Advertiſement, and all Officers, Civil and Military, and all other Perſons are hereby required at their peril to aſſiſt the Continental Officers in carrying the ſame into Execution. By order of the COUNCIL, and Aſſembly,

M. WEARE, Preſident.
JOHN LANGDON, Speaker.

A public notice promising pardons to all soldiers absent from the Continental Army provided they rejoin their regiments within a month.

his fine home in August 1765, the "Boston Massacre" (inspired phrase of Samuel Adams) in 1770, and the "Boston Tea Party" in 1773. Finally Britain closed the port of Boston because its citizens refused to pay for the destroyed tea. The city was then occupied by British troops.

In contrast to Massachusetts Bay, New Hampshire was predominantly loyal. Its relations with England had always been peaceful, even pleasant. The colonial authorities in England had dealt more gently with New Hampshire than with recalcitrant Massachusetts Bay. Like Boston, Portsmouth had its Sons of Liberty and shouting tavern heroes, but hardworking and practical New Hampshire was always more concerned with everyday matters than with political affairs. People liked Governor John Wentworth and approved his actions. In the late 1760's and early 1770's New Hampshire was content to let well enough alone. Revolutionary sentiment might well have subsided in the province after the repeal of the Stamp Act had it not been whipped into fury in Boston and spread out from there.

New Hampshire Committed

Yet what has been called the first overt act of resistance took place in New Hampshire.

In July 1774, a Provincial Congress met at Exeter and named John Sullivan and Nathaniel Folsom delegates from New Hampshire to the Continental Congress in Philadelphia. On December 15, 1774, a force of some four hundred men led by Sullivan and John Langdon, a young Portsmouth merchant, attacked Fort William and Mary at Newcastle. The fort was defended by only one officer, Captain John Cochran, and five soldiers. This tiny garrison tried to defend itself and got off one volley of its three 4-pound cannon before the attackers swarmed into the fort from all sides. They took the defenders prisoner and held them for about an hour and a half while they broke out the store of arms and ammunition, taking cannon, small arms, and a hundred barrels of gunpowder. They hid them in Durham near Sullivan's home in preparation for the war they were certain was coming. It was these stores that the patriots used in the Battle of Bunker Hill.

Three days later, Governor John Wentworth, who had been counseling moderation, wrote General Thomas Gage, governor of Massachusetts Bay, "This day the town is full of armed men, who refuse to disperse, but appear determined to complete the dismantling of the fort entirely." He said that if he had two hundred men he might be able to restore order, but he did not have them.

At the Second Provincial Congress in Exeter, Colonel Nathaniel Weare and the Reverend Paine Wingate tried to make moderate views prevail, but they were shouted down. Langdon and Sullivan dominated the Congress, which voted to raise soldiers, arms, and supplies. Judge Nathaniel Weare was made chairman of the Committee of Safety that was to rule New Hampshire throughout the Revolution. As Portsmouth was too closely connected with the royal government, Exeter was made the working capital of New Hampshire.

It was not until the fight at Concord, Massachusetts, in 1775 that New Hampshire really took fire. Some of its Indian war veterans fought there. By June 1, 1775, more than two thousand New Hampshire soldiers in three regiments were with the colonial forces which General George Washington had assembled at Cambridge and was training for the assault on British-held Boston.

As in the other colonies, particularly Massachusetts Bay, hatred of those who did not quickly and loudly declare for the cause was unrestrained. Tories or those suspected of loyalist sympathies were imprisoned and their property confiscated. Some managed to flee to Nova Scotia or to England or to join the British in Boston. As Belknap put it a few years later:

> The passions of jealousy, hatred and revenge were freely indulged, and the tongue of slander was under no restraint. Wise and good men secretly lamented these excesses; but no effectual remedy could be administered. All commissions under the former authority being annulled, the courts of justice were shut, and the sword of magistracy was sheathed. The Provincial Congress directed the general affairs of the war; and the town committees had a discretionary but undefined power to preserve domestic peace. Habits of decency, family government, and the good example of influential persons, contributed more to maintain order than any other authority.

Mob Violence

As their revolutionary ardor was inflamed, people tore down or defaced every sign bearing the royal arms, scepters, crowns, and other insignia of British rule. Families had to conceal prized pictures and coats of arms which they had once proudly displayed. Street names with English origins were changed. Halfpence that carried the likeness of King George III were refused in trade or accepted at only half their value.

Early in June 1775, a mob descended on the home of New Hampshire's Governor John Wentworth demanding that he surrender to them a former British army captain who was his guest. The governor and his family escaped the back way through the gardens to the South Mill Pond and were taken to Fort William and Mary by boat while the mob ransacked the mansion. The Wentworths sailed aboard a British man-of-war for Boston. When Boston was evacuated, they escaped to Halifax with thousands of other loyalists and in 1778 sailed to England. Wentworth's property, including his Wolfeborough estate, was confiscated.

In 1792 John Wentworth was made lieutenant governor of Nova Scotia. He was knighted in 1795. As Sir John Wentworth, he held his post in Nova Scotia for sixteen years. There, as he had done in New Hampshire, he improved roads and transport and was active in developing educational facilities.

New Hampshire at Bunker Hill

John Stark had been commissioned a militia colonel by the first Provincial Congress. He was at his mill in Dumbarton when news of the

John Stark

fighting at Concord, Massachusetts, reached him. Ten minutes later he was riding for Medford, Massachusetts, where he had directed his New Hampshire volunteers to assemble.

Stark was of medium height with bold features, tight lips, and light-blue eyes. He had been hardened by his Ranger service and was a fighter who brooked no nonsense from the enemy or even from his own army. The paymaster of the New Hampshire troops did not like Stark and tried to cause disaffection among the men, who were on a six months' enlistment. He told them that their pay vouchers were not properly filled out. The men marched away and returned with the vouchers presumably correct. The paymaster refused them a second, then a third time. At Medford the angry Stark had the paymaster arrested and brought to his camp. He said the vouchers were correct, and saw to it that his men were paid. Stark's unorthodox conduct was investigated, but meanwhile the paymaster found himself under suspicion as a defaulter and quit the army.

Stark and his men, including an entire company of volunteers from his native Londonderry, fought tenaciously at Bunker Hill. In this crucial battle of June 17, 1775, which was so costly a victory for the British, two thirds of the American troops were from New Hampshire. When the Americans were forced to withdraw from Bunker Hill, Stark had the British dead piled before his lines to cover the retreat. In the midst of the fight word was brought to Stark that his sixteen-year-old son had been killed. He told the messenger that it was no time to talk of private affairs, and ordered him back to his post. The report proved false; Stark's son served throughout the war as a staff officer.

The New Hampshire Declaration

Even after Concord and Bunker Hill, New Hampshire felt that it was fighting for a redress of wrongs, not for political severance from England. Later in 1775, the Fifth Provincial Congress in Exeter declared in a statement, actually not issued until January 5, 1776:

> That we never sought to throw off our dependence upon Great Britain but felt ourselves happy under her protection,

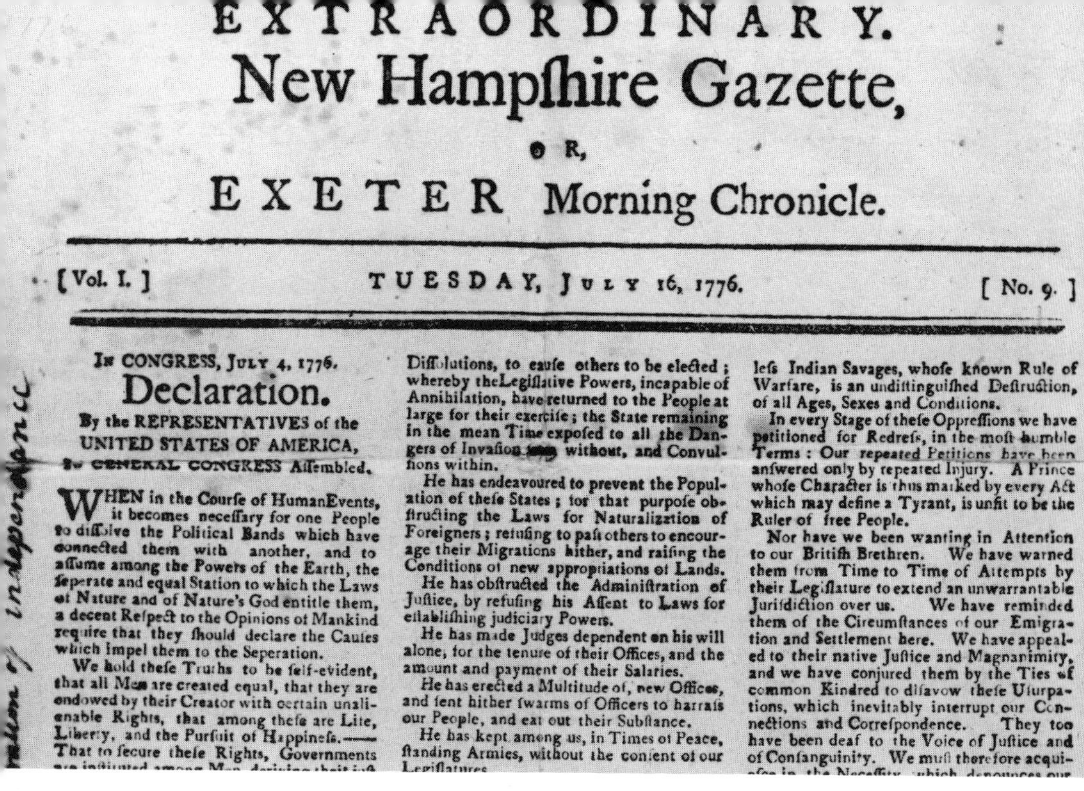

EXTRAORDINARY.

New Hampshire Gazette,

OR,

EXETER Morning Chronicle.

[Vol. I.] TUESDAY, JULY 16, 1776. [No. 9.]

IN CONGRESS, JULY 4, 1776.

Declaration.

By the REPRESENTATIVES of the UNITED STATES OF AMERICA, In GENERAL CONGRESS Assembled.

WHEN in the Course of Human Events, it becomes necessary for one People to dissolve the Political Bands which have connected them with another, and to assume among the Powers of the Earth, the seperate and equal Station to which the Laws of Nature and of Nature's God entitle them, a decent Respect to the Opinions of Mankind require that they should declare the Causes which impel them to the Seperation.

We hold these Truths to be self-evident, that all Men are created equal, that they are endowed by their Creator with certain unalienable Rights, that among these are Life, Liberty, and the Pursuit of Happiness.—— That to secure these Rights, Governments

Dissolutions, to cause others to be elected; whereby the Legislative Powers, incapable of Annihilation, have returned to the People at large for their exercise; the State remaining in the mean Time exposed to all the Dangers of Invasion without, and Convulsions within.

He has endeavoured to prevent the Population of these States; for that purpose obstructing the Laws for Naturalization of Foreigners; refusing to pass others to encourage their Migrations hither, and raising the Conditions of new appropriations of Lands.

He has obstructed the Administration of Justice, by refusing his Assent to Laws for establishing judiciary Powers.

He has made Judges dependent on his will alone, for the tenure of their Offices, and the amount and payment of their Salaries.

He has erected a Multitude of new Offices, and sent hither swarms of Officers to harrass our People, and eat out their Substance.

He has kept among us, in Times of Peace, standing Armies, without the consent of our Legislatures

less Indian Savages, whose known Rule of Warfare, is an undistinguished Destruction, of all Ages, Sexes and Conditions.

In every Stage of these Oppressions we have petitioned for Redress, in the most humble Terms: Our repeated Petitions have been answered only by repeated Injury. A Prince whose Character is thus marked by every Act which may define a Tyrant, is unfit to be the Ruler of free People.

Nor have we been wanting in Attention to our British Brethren. We have warned them from Time to Time of Attempts by their Legislature to extend an unwarrantable Jurisdiction over us. We have reminded them of the Circumstances of our Emigration and Settlement here. We have appealed to their native Justice and Magnanimity, and we have conjured them by the Ties of common Kindred to disavow these Usurpations, which inevitably interrupt our Connections and Correspondence. They too have been deaf to the Voice of Justice and of Consanguinity. We must therefore acqui-

Copy of the Declaration of Independence as printed in the *New Hampshire Gazette* on July 16, 1776.

> while we could enjoy our constitutional rights and privileges; and that we shall rejoice if such a reconciliation between us and our parent State can be effected as shall be approved by the Continental Congress in whose prudence and wisdom we confide.

Leaders of what still considered itself a province of England continued to hope for retention of the status it had long enjoyed. But as the war progressed, their attitude changed, and John Langdon forcibly stated before the New Hampshire General Assembly:

> I have three thousand dollars in hard money. I will pledge my plate for three thousand more. I have seventy hogsheads of Tobago rum, which shall be sold for the most it will bring. These are at the service of the state. If we succeed in defending our firesides and our homes, I may be remunerated; if we

> do not, the property will be of no value to me. Our old friend Stark, who so nobly defended the honor of our state at Bunker's Hill, may be safely entrusted with the conduct of the enterprise, and we will check the progress of Burgoyne.

Determination hardening, New Hampshire issued its Declaration of Independence, the first statement of separation from Great Britain, three weeks before the Continental Congress proclaimed the independence of the United Colonies. The New Hampshire General Assembly said:

> We do hereby declare that it is the opinion of this assembly that our delegates at the Continental Congress shall be instructed, to join with the other colonies in declaring the thirteen United Colonies a free and independent State, solemnly pledging our faith and honor that we will, on our part, support the measure with our lives and fortunes; and that, in consequence thereof, they, the Continental Congress, on whose wisdom, fidelity, and integrity we rely, may enter into and form such alliances as they may judge conducive to the present safety and future advantage of these American colonies; provided that regulation of our internal policies be under the jurisdiction of this Assembly.

The Battle of Bennington

Langdon's trust in John Stark was well placed.

In the north the colonial forces had been in wide retreat before the advancing British. After the siege of Boston, Colonel Stark had gone to Canada and served with the Americans on their retreat south. He fought later in the battles of Trenton and Princeton in New Jersey, but resigned his commission in March 1777, because Congress, considering him willful and too apt to act on his own, had promoted junior officers over his head.

When General John Burgoyne invaded Vermont, the authorities there appealed to New Hampshire for aid. Stark was commissioned a New Hampshire brigadier general. In a short time he raised and equipped an army of 1,400 men and marched them over the mountains to Manchester, Vermont. On August 8, 1777, he moved his men south to Bennington to cooperate with General Schuyler in harassing Burgoyne's flank. Disregarding Schuyler's orders to join him in retreat, Stark attacked a German force of 500 to 700 men under the command of Colonel Baum, who had been sent to take the horses, wagons, and supplies supposed to be at Bennington.

Stark's New Hampshire troops, augmented by volunteers from the Berkshires in Massachusetts, fell on the Germans from all sides. They ran up to the enemy artillerymen and killed them before they could fire their cannon. Baum himself was killed in a charge, and his force surrendered. When another officer came up with reinforcements, Stark turned the captured English cannon on him and his Brunswick mercenaries.

This battle, fought by New Hampshire men and some Massachusetts volunteers a few miles above Bennington, actually took place in New York. It was an important victory, for it helped stem the invasion of the British from the north and resulted in the ultimate defeat of Burgoyne's army at Saratoga. Total loss to the British, including those captured, was put at 700, while the Americans had only 70 men killed or wounded.

Still smarting from what he considered unjust treatment and with the excuse that his commission was from New Hampshire, General Stark did not report his success to the Continental Congress, which had started to investigate his disobedience of Schuyler's order to retreat. Congress dropped the charges and resolved instead: "That the thanks of the Congress be presented to General Stark of the New Hampshire militia, and the officers and troops under his command, for their brave and successful attack upon and the victory over the enemy in their lines at Bennington; and that Brigadier Stark is to be appointed a Brigadier-General in the armies of the United States."

Mollified by this promotion, Stark went on to capture Fort Edward and to ensure the surrender of Burgoyne by cutting off his line of retreat across the Hudson. A plainspoken combat soldier, General John Stark was New Hampshire's popular hero during the Revolution. His name drew willing volunteers to fight under him.

Stark served with Gates in Rhode Island in 1779 and at the battle of Springfield in 1780. In 1781 he was made commander in chief of the Department of the North, and he was promoted to major general in September 1783. Stark served unscathed throughout the war, then retired to his large estates. He lived to be ninety-four years old and was buried on his own land in May 1822.

New Hampshire Privateers

New Hampshire was the only one of the thirteen colonies that was not invaded during the Revolution. This was due partly to the geography of the war, but it has been ascribed as well to the fearsome reputation of her fighting men. They fought all through the war, New Hampshire having as many as 4,000 men in the army at the same time. Another 3,000 New Hampshire men sailed on privateers preying on British ships. After 1776 as many as 100 privateers of eight to ten guns operated out of Portsmouth, cruising from Nova Scotia to the West Indies, and even crossing the Atlantic to harass British shipping in the English Channel and the North Sea.

On April 3, 1776, John Jay, as president of the Continental Congress, issued "Instructions to the Commanders of Private Ships, or Vessels of War, which shall have Commissions or Letters of Marque and Reprisal, authorizing them to make Capture of British Vessels or Cargoes." Privateers were authorized to attack any English ship, bring it into any colonial port, and have its master, pilot, and other "principal persons" tried before the courts. They were forbidden to destroy, sell, or waste any captured cargo until a properly authorized court declared it a lawful prize. One third of a privateer's complement had to be "land-men"—that is, fighters—but Jay's instructions warned sternly, "If you, or any of your officers or crew, shall, in cold blood, kill or maim, or by Torture or otherwise, cruelly, inhumanely, and contrary to common Usage and the Practice of civilized Nations in war, treat any Person or Persons surprised in the Ship or Vessel you shall take, the Offender shall be severely punished."

That these restrictions were closely followed is doubtful. The risks

John Sullivan

and rewards in privateering were both high. If captured, privateer sailors could be hanged. More often they were impressed into the British navy or flung into prison.

If they were not caught or killed, privateersmen could do very well. The master of the *General Sullivan* got £36,793 as his share of a single prize in 1780, and even his ordinary seamen got rich on their shares.

Portsmouth also built and fitted the navy vessel *Ranger* for John Paul Jones and even provided most of its officers and crew.

General John Sullivan

Owen O'Sullivan, aged thirty-one, emigrated from Limerick, Ireland, in 1723. He changed his name to John Sullivan, paid the passage of an attractive Irish girl named Margery Brown, who came as an indentured servant, and married her. Sulllivan was a farmer, but in the winter he taught Latin and Greek in the towns near Portsmouth. He and his sharp-spoken wife had four sons, but the course of true love did not run smooth, and Sullivan fled to Boston to escape his wife. Little daunted, Margery Sullivan advertised for his return in the *Boston Evening Post*, of July 25, 1743. She admitted that she had been "too rash and unadvised" in her speech to him but asked, "Why should a few angry and unkind words from an angry and fretful wife, for which I am now paying full dear, make you thus forsake me and your children?" John Sullivan returned.

The Sullivans' first child, another John Sullivan, had been born in 1740. He studied law under Samuel Livermore in Portsmouth and became an eloquent, argumentative, and litigious New Hampshire attorney and instinctively a politician. In 1772 he was appointed a major in the New Hampshire militia. Probably in part as recognition of his exploit at Fort William and Mary, he was made a brigadier general by the Continental Congress, to which he was a delegate from New Hampshire.

As a soldier, Sullivan is said to have been brave, impetuous, and fond of display. He was in Washington's army at Boston and then with the northern army on its retreat south, and became a major general on August 9, 1776. He was captured by the British on Long Island and sent by Lord Howe to try to negotiate peace with the Continental Congress in Philadelphia.

Sullivan rejoined the American forces at Princeton and Trenton. With other American officers he threatened to resign if Congress kept promoting French officers over his head. He did not resign, but he failed in a mission to capture Staten Island in New York harbor, and his conduct at the Battle of the Brandywine in Pennsylvania was called into question. Enemies in Congress moved to suspend him from command; but Washington refused, and Sullivan was exonerated. An action in Rhode Island where Sullivan cooperated with the French fleet also failed. Angered, General Sullivan resigned his commission and returned to Congress.

New Hampshire had other notable Revolutionary soldiers. Colonel, later Major General, Jonathan Cilley, Colonel Henry Dearborn, a physician of Nottingham Square, Colonel James Read, who led a regiment at Bunker Hill, and Colonel, then Brigadier, Alexander Scammel were among them. Scammel, a young Harvard graduate who had studied law with Sullivan in Portsmouth, was killed at Yorktown.

One New Hampshire soldier, Ebenezer Webster of Salisbury, was captain of the guard at West Point the night after the defection of Benedict Arnold. The legend is that Washington saw him and said, "Ah, Captain, I know I can trust you and your men from New Hampshire."

The Loyalists

The Revolution, like the Civil War, sometimes broke up families and set brother against brother. William Stark had been, along with his brother, a Ranger officer. He had helped capture Ticonderoga and Crown Point and served under Amherst in the second siege of Louisburg. Feeling bound by his king's commission, which both brothers held, he remained loyal to England and tried, but obviously failed, to change John Stark's views. William Stark was prescribed as a Tory, and his property was seized. He returned to active duty in the royal army, became a colonel, and fought on Long Island, where he was killed in a fall from his horse.

Robert Rogers himself vacillated for a time. Returning to America in 1776, he tried for preferment in both the British and the American armies. His actions were such that George Washington became exasperated with him and had him imprisoned as a spy. Rogers escaped and joined the British as a lieutenant colonel commissioned to raise a force of Rangers. Rogers recruited the men, but this was another war, and tactics had changed. His Rangers were defeated at White Plains, New York, and Rogers was relieved of command and ordered to recruiting duty. Dishonesty, reckless behavior, and dissipation ended that assignment. Rogers fled to England in 1780 and, still on half pay as a major in the royal army, lived about fifteen years longer. He died in a London lodging house.

Count Rumford

The zeal of inquisitorial New Hampshire patriots drove one of the most brilliant men in the province to the side of the enemy.

Son of Captain Ebenezer Thompson, who had distinguished himself in the French and Indian War, Benjamin Thompson was born in Woburn in Massachusetts Bay in 1753. He showed an early aptitude for science and mathematics and, supported by a small inheritance from his grandfather, attended lectures at Harvard in astronomy and higher mathematics while studying medicine with Dr. John Hay of Woburn. He then went to Rumford, New Hampshire, to teach school.

In November 1772, Thompson married the widow (a daughter of the Reverend Timothy Walker) of the wealthy Colonel Benjamin Rolfe, and they went to Portsmouth on their wedding journey. Thompson was six feet tall and had ingratiating manners. Impressed by his handsome appearance, his grace and charm, and particularly his seat on a horse, Governor John Wentworth immediately made him a major in the Second Provincial Regiment of New Hampshire. This favor aroused the jealousy of other militia officers.

From the start of his unusual career, Thompson had made it a habit to cultivate the great, and he received many favors from them. Although he usually made enemies in the process, he gratified his ambitions.

For two years Thompson ran his wife's estate and experimented with gunpowder. Their only child, Sarah, was born October 17, 1774, but the following May her parents separated, never to see each other again.

In the eyes of zealous patriots the patronage of Governor Wentworth made Benjamin Thompson a loyalist. In 1774 he was summoned before a committee in Rumford and charged with "being unfriendly to the cause of Liberty." The charge was dismissed for lack of evidence, but Thompson was publicly threatened with bodily harm if he remained in the town. He returned to Woburn, where he was quickly arrested again on a similar charge.

Thompson then applied at Cambridge for a commission in Washington's army, but it was denied, probably because of the jealousy of New Hampshire officers. Rebuffed, Thompson sailed for England, where he quickly found favor. He was given a post in the colonial office, then made secretary of the province of Georgia. About 1781 he was commissioned lieutenant colonel in the royal army and served the next year near Charleston, South Carolina. Later he assumed command of a regiment on Long Island. On his return to England—where he was already a Fellow of the Royal Society for his work on cohesion—Thompson was made colonel of the newly organized King's American Dragoons.

Thompson's spectacular career as a scientist, soldier, and statesman was only beginning. He was knighted in England, and the Elector of Bavaria, whom he served as major general and adviser, made him a count of the Holy Roman Empire. Thompson chose the title of Count Rumford after the town that had expelled him. In addition Poland bestowed upon him the Order of Saint Stanislaus.

In England, to which he returned in 1795, Count Rumford developed improvements in heating and cooking. The Royal Society honored him for humanitarian services there and in Germany and Ireland. In London he served as minister plenipotentiary of Bavaria.

The United States offered Count Rumford both the superintendency of its new military academy at West Point and the job of inspecting the artillery of the United States Army, but he was too busy with the affairs of the Royal Institution for the Diffusion of Scientific Knowledge to leave London. When he did leave, it was to live in Paris with his daughter. When Count Rumford died in 1814, his will established a chair of science at Harvard College.

Paul Wentworth

Paul Wentworth was a near relative of Governor John Wentworth, who thought highly of his abilities and got him appointed to the council of New Hampshire. In the early 1770's he served as agent for the province in London, but he lived in many places, for Paul Wentworth was something of an eighteenth-century cosmopolite. He was also a speculator and financial manipulator. He had land in New Hampshire, had lived for a time in the West Indies, and had a plantation in Surinam, on the northeast coast of South America.

During the American Revolution, Paul Wentworth was a high-echelon British spy. As a member of the Secret Service he directed a network of spies, among them double agent Edward Bancroft of Westfield, Massachusetts. Under various aliases and in various disguises, Wentworth himself often visited the Continent. Daring and alert, he tried his best to keep France from entering the war on the side of the colonies, and he warned George III of the dangers in a possible Franco-American alliance. The King ignored his warnings.

At another point in the war Wentworth worked through Silas Deane and the wily Benjamin Franklin, whose complete confidence Bancroft had obtained, to effect a reconciliation between Great Britain and the colonies on England's terms. Wentworth hoped for a knighthood and a lucrative political appointment as a reward for his services to England, but George III distrusted him because of his stock gambling. Wentworth did obtain a seat in Parliament in 1780, but his term was short. He remained in London speculating and pursuing office until 1790, when he returned to Surinam.

Samuel Livermore

Some leading men of New Hampshire found themselves in an embarrassing position. That their abilities had brought them high office in the provincial government was now their chief liability. Some managed to survive the change and attained positions of leadership under the new order. One of these men was Samuel Livermore.

A Princeton (College of New Jersey) graduate, Livermore was a forceful and effective lawyer. He became judge advocate of the Admiralty Court in New Hampshire, then attorney general of the province. After a dispute with Governor Wentworth, he moved from Portsmouth to Londonderry and represented New Hampshire in the General Assembly, but he continued to hold his royal office. He became a great landowner, acquiring ten to twelve thousand acres and building a large mansion in Holderness.

All this, even though Livermore proclaimed his adherence to the cause of independence, was enough to condemn him in the eyes of most patriots. He was out of office for several years, and during that time worked a grist mill on his property with his own hands. He then got back into the Assembly as a member from Holderness and back into power through the help of Meshech Weare and others at Exeter who knew his worth. By 1778 Samuel Livermore, this time under the Revolutionary government, was once again attorney general of New Hampshire.

After the Revolution, Livermore—who happened to be a brother-in-law of Robert Rogers—became a distinguished figure in New Hampshire, serving three terms in the United States Congress and two in the Senate.

President (Governor) Meshech Weare

In New Hampshire there was very nearly a hereditary political aristocracy among the Whigs, as there had been among the Tory Wentworths and their patrician kin.

The first Nathaniel Weare settled in Newbury in 1638. His son was the Nathaniel Weare who had opposed Lieutenant Governor Cranfield and was attorney for William Vaughan. To prevent Cranfield from getting some of the Hampton town records, he took them with him when he went to England as agent for those who petitioned against Cranfield's misrule. On his return from his successful mission, he was rewarded by the four towns—and fined £50 for embezzlement.

The second Nathaniel Weare was made chief justice of New Hampshire in April 1694. His son, Meshech Weare, was born in 1713 and graduated from Harvard in 1735. Meshech Weare had planned to enter the ministry, but instead he became an attorney and went into public affairs. At the outbreak of the Revolution he was a militia colonel, a member of the General Assembly, and a Superior Court Judge.

A conservative, Weare was slow to accept the revolutionary idea, but once the war started he became the leading civilian in New Hampshire and was president of its Council throughout the Revolution. Weare was a calm, steady man with a penetrating intelligence. He lived on his farm at Hampton Falls and made the seven-mile trip into Exeter daily, even when he was in his sixties. Weare was the indispensable man in New Hampshire and the trusted ally of George Washington, with whom he was in constant communication.

When, after several false starts, New Hampshire adopted a state constitution in 1783, Meshech Weare was made the first president of the state, the title "governor" not yet having come into use.

The New Hampshire Constitution

A constitution framed in 1779 had been presented to but rejected by the people of New Hampshire. A new constitutional convention was held in Concord in 1781. After long consideration it prepared a document modeled after the constitution of Massachusetts. This constitution provided for a house and senate; every member of the house had to have an estate worth £100, while a Senate member had to be worth £200. Property qualifications were also established for voters. The pay of legislators was set at sixteen shillings a day. This state constitution was adopted in 1783 and went into effect as of 1784.

The Treaty of Paris

The Treaty of Paris, signed September 3, 1783, brought an end to the eight years of war that had really ended with the defeat of Lord Cornwallis at Yorktown, Virginia, in October 1781. The treaty recognized the independence of what had been England's colonies in North America and set the boundaries of the new country.

There was a full day of celebration in Portsmouth when peace was declared. It began with a salute of thirteen guns at six o'clock in the morning. Crowds attended religious services of thanksgiving at the North Church. The president and other chief officers of New Hampshire were present as the proclamation was read by the sheriff of Rockingham. State dignitaries and gentlemen of the town banqueted and drank rounds of toasts. In the evening there was a great ball, with fireworks and the illumination of the State House.

With the twelve other colonies that now were states, New Hampshire had something to celebrate. It was a new political entity in a new country, and the possibilities for the future were boundless. But the present was nothing to celebrate at all.

The condition of New Hampshire, which had about 140,000 people at this point, was dismal and for many people desperate. New Hampshire had lost many men. It was virtually bankrupt, unable to pay the taxes leveled by the Confederated government. There was little hard money, and the Continental currency had so depreciated that £40 was worth only £1. Trade had fallen off badly. Portsmouth had lost most of its shipping. Education had been neglected during the war—to the point of extinction in many towns. Even Dartmouth College had languished.

Postwar Rebellion

Even when they plied other trades or professions, most New Hampshire men were farmers. But although the land was fertile and most people lived well, many were poor. Officers and men who had survived the war were without funds, and many could not go back to their former occupations. Even some men who had been wealthy were in debt. There was sharp resentment against the courts, the lawyers, and what moneylenders there were. Fierce demands were made for a more stable currency. Those in distress were encouraged by some who had been their wartime leaders to revolt.

Angry mobs of men from many towns started for Exeter, where the legislature was in session in September 1786. The mob reached the town on the evening of the twentieth and demanded that paper money equal to the state debt be issued. General John Sullivan, who had succeeded the aging Meshech Weare as president of New Hampshire, confronted the men and talked to them to gain time while his forces were alerted. With the consent of both houses of the legislature, Sullivan ordered all militia commanders out with their companies. About two thousand armed soldiers under Major General Cilley and volunteers under Nicholas Gilman were marshaled and reached Exeter by the morning of the twenty-first.

Faced by such decisive action and so formidable a force, the rebels gave way. They were driven off without a shot being fired, and their leaders were arrested.

Adoption of the Federal Constitution

Slowly New Hampshire began to recover from exhaustion and depletion. Men returned to their farms, and their farms responded to the attention they had lacked during the war. New settlers pushed farther up into the valleys and the mountain intervales and cleared new land. Towns grew, though some, like Portsmouth and Londonderry, would never fully regain their lost strength and importance.

With concerns of its own, New Hampshire was cautious in its dealings with the other states and about its participation in the formation of the United States.

General Sullivan was chairman of the convention that met in June 1788 to consider adoption of the Federal Constitution. In general, New Hampshire sentiment as expressed by most of its leading politicians was against adoption. They felt that the constitution framed by the Federal Constitutional Convention in Philadelphia a year before had granted too much power to a central government. New Hampshire had been fighting its own battles and doing its best to govern itself for a long time, and the delegates were reluctant to commit it again to outside control.

It looked very much as if the convention would reject the plan offered when Colonel Ebenezer Webster, the same militia officer to whom Washington had spoken at West Point, asked permission to speak. Webster had been one of the founders of Salisbury, where for many years he had served as selectman and town clerk. He had been given 225 acres on the upper Merrimack for his services under General Amherst, and he had fought through the Revolution. He was a member of the New Hampshire senate and would eventually become a judge of the Court of Common Pleas. On this occasion Webster said:

> *Mr. President:* I have listened to the arguments for and against the Constitution. I am convinced such a government as that constitution will establish, if adopted—a government acting directly on the people of the States—is necessary for the common defence and the general welfare. It is the only government which will enable us to pay off the national debt—the debt which we owe for the Revolution, and which we are bound in honor fully and fairly to discharge. Besides, I have followed the lead of Washington through seven years of war, and I have never been misled. His name is subscribed to this constitution. He will not mislead us now. I shall vote for its adoption.

Colonel Ebenezer Webster was the father of Daniel Webster who, as everyone knows, drove the Devil from New Hampshire. The colonel's plea was convincing, but it was a narrow squeak. New Hampshire adopted the Federal Constitution by a vote of 57 to 47.

As it turned out, New Hampshire's vote was crucial. The ninth state to accept the Constitution, it provided the two-thirds majority needed. The United States of America under the Constitution was now a fact.

When the Federal Constitution was adopted, there was a huge celebration in Portsmouth, still New Hampshire's principal town, though no longer its capital. On June 26, 1788, people poured in from the surrounding towns and countryside to see the great parade there. A band in an open coach drawn by six horses was followed by a procession of all the trades: reapers, haymakers, threshers, blacksmiths, sailors, caulkers, shipwrights, rope makers, judges, tailors, barbers, hat makers, and others.

Each craft carried its tools or instruments. The nautical instrument makers bore an azimuth compass, pilots their glasses and charts; boat builders were at work on a boat. The good ship *Union*, manned, rigged, and armed, was elevated on a dray drawn by nine horses. The militia paraded in full uniform, and as the procession moved along, printers turned out copies of patriotic songs. Their display bore a motto:

> A government of freemen never knows
> A tyrant's shackles, on the press t'impose.

Washington's Visit

When he paid a state visit to New Hampshire the next year, President George Washington was met at the state line by the president and council of New Hampshire, together with many mounted gentlemen. He was escorted into Portsmouth by a troop of New Hampshire cavalry while other military units drew up in salute along the way.

When Washington reached the center of Portsmouth, three companies of artillery loosed a 13-gun salute. Once more Congress Street was lined with men arranged by trades. Bands played and odes were sung as General Sullivan introduced the President of the United States to the cheering crowds. There were three whole days of parades and displays, of music and fireworks for George Washington, who was entertained, of course, in the resplendent mansion in which Benning and then John Wentworth had lived as governors of the English royal province that was now the State of New Hampshire.

Important Dates

1623	Founding of New Hampshire
1635	Death of Captain John Mason
1638	Associations for town government in Portsmouth, Dover, and Exeter
1641–1679	Union with Massachusetts Bay
1675–1676	King Phillip's War
1680	Establishment of the Royal Province of New Hampshire
1682–1685	Edward Cranfield lieutenant governor
1685	Walter Barefoot deputy governor
1686–1689	New Hampshire part of Dominion of New England
1689–1697	King William's War
1689–1690	Reversion to separate town governments
1690–1692	Second union with Massachusetts Bay
1692–1775	Royal Province of New Hampshire
1701–1713	Queen Anne's War
1717–1729	John Wentworth lieutenant governor
1719	Founding of Londonderry
1725	Founding of Rumford (Concord)
1741	Boundary between New Hampshire and Massachusetts Bay fixed
1741–1767	Benning Wentworth governor
1744–1748	King George's War
1754–1762	French and Indian War
1767–1775	Sir John Wentworth governor
1770	Founding of Dartmouth College in Hanover
1774	Seizure of arms and ammunition at Fort William and Mary
1775	New Hampshire at the battle of Bunker Hill
1777	Battle of Bennington
1781	Founding of Phillips Academy, Exeter
1783	Adoption of constitution of State of New Hampshire
1788	Adoption of constitution of the United States

Bibliography

Adams, Nathaniel, *Annals of Portsmouth*. Portsmouth, N.H.: Published by the author, 1825.

Alden, Lucius, *Historical Discourse*. Portsmouth, N.H.: C. W. Brewster, 1849.

Barstow, George, *The History of New Hampshire, from its Discovery to the Passage of the Toleration Act, in 1819*. Concord, N.H.: I. S. Boyd, June 4, 1842.

Belknap, Jeremy, *The History of New-Hampshire*, 3 vols., 2nd ed. Boston: Bradford and Read, 1813.

Bouton, Nathaniel, *The History of Concord*. Concord, N.H.: Benning W. Sanborn, 1856.

Collections of the New-Hampshire Historical Society

Vol. 1 for the year 1824. Concord, N.H.: Jacob B. Moore, 1824.

Vol. 3 Concord, N.H.: Jacob B. Moore, 1832.

Vol. 6 Concord, N.H.: Asa McFarland, 1850.

Vol. 8, ed. Nathaniel Bouton. Concord, N.H.: McFarland & Jenks, 1866.

Dictionary of American Biography, centenary edition. New York: Charles Scribner's Sons, 1946.

Dow, Joseph A. M., *Historical Address*. Concord, N.H.: Asa McFarland, February 1839.

Everett, Edward, *Life of John Stark*. New York: Harper & Brothers, 1834.

Faulkner, Harold Underwood, *American Economic History*, 9th ed. New York: Harper & Brothers, 1943.

Fiske, John, *The Beginnings of New England*. Boston and New York: Houghton, Mifflin and Co., 1889.

Hawthorne, Julian, *The History of the United States*, 3 vols. New York: P. F. Collier & Son, 1912.

McClintock, John N., *History of New Hampshire*. Boston: B. B. Russell, 1888.

Mason, John, *A Briefe Discourse of the New-found-land*. Edinburgh: Andro Hart, 1620.

Capt. John Mason. The Publications of the Prince Society, Vol. 17. Boston: John Wilson and Son, 1887.

New Hampshire, A Guide to the Granite State. American Guide Series, Federal Writers' Project. Boston: Houghton Mifflin Co., 1938.

Parker, Edward L., *Century Sermon*. Concord, N.H.: George Hough, 1819.

Penhallow, Samuel, *The History of the Wars of New-England with the Eastern Indians*. Boston: T. Fleet, 1726.

Pillsbury, Hobart, *New Hampshire: Resources, Attractions, and Its People*, vol. 1. New York: The Lewis Historical Publishing Co., Inc., 1927.

Roberts, Kenneth, *Northwest Passage*. Garden City, N.Y.: Doubleday, Doran & Co., 1936, 1937.

Sanborn, Frank B., *New Hampshire, An Epitome of Popular Government*. Boston: Houghton, Mifflin and Co., 1904.

Spalding, George B., *Historical Discourse*. Dover, N.H.: Morning Star Job Printing Office, 1881.

Sylvester, Herbert Milton, *Indian Wars of New England*, 3 vols. Boston: W. B. Clarke Co., 1910.

Wissler, Clark, *Indians of the United States*, rev. ed. New York: Doubleday & Co., 1966.

Historic Sites

AMHERST

Birthplace of Horace Greeley, February 3, 1811.

CONCORD

At 30 Park Street close to New Hampshire Capitol, the New Hampshire Historical Society. In addition to its reference library and its collection of the papers of Daniel Webster, Franklin Pierce, and other New Hampshire notables, the society has an extensive collection of New Hampshire artifacts. Its Prentis Collection is a series of rooms—dining room, parlor, bedroom, and kitchen—designed and furnished as they might have been in the home of a prosperous New Hampshire merchant of the early eighteenth century. On display in the rotunda of the building is a restored Concord coach, one of those made in Concord in the midnineteenth century by the Abbot Downing Company. The Concord coach was the Wells Fargo stagecoach of the American West. At nearby Penacook is the Hannah Dustin monument, commemorating the exploit of 1697 in which she slew her Indian captors.

CHARLESTOWN

Restoration here of Number 4, the fort built in 1745, which guarded the New Hampshire frontier during the French and Indian War. Built with funds donated from private organizations and maintained by a nonprofit corporation, Old Number 4 has five log buildings within its log stockade: the Great Hall with its watch tower, Hastings House, Captain Stevens' house, Parker-Sartwell building, and Lieutenant Moses Willard house. A twenty-minute color slide and taped narration tell the history of the fort in a little theater under the Great Hall. Indian artifacts and colonial military equipment are on exhibit.

DOVER

At the Woodman Institute are the Dame Garrison house, circa 1675, and the John Parker Hale house.

DURHAM

The home of Revolutionary Major General John Sullivan, who later became president of New Hampshire.

EXETER

Capital of New Hampshire during the Revolution. The Gilman-Ladd house is headquarters of the New Hampshire Society of the Cincinnati. Phillips Academy, founded during the Revolution, is in Exeter.

FRANKLIN (between Franklin and Salisbury).

The birthplace, January 18, 1782, and boyhood home of Daniel Webster. Partially restored and period furnished.

HAMPTON

Winnacunnet Plantation, an historical restoration.

Hanover

Dartmouth Hall is a replica of the original building of Dartmouth College, founded in 1769.

Hillsboro

The Franklin Pierce homestead, where the fourteenth President of the United States was born November 23, 1804.

New Castle (Great Island).

Portions of old Fort William and Mary remain.

Portsmouth and vicinity.

The provincial capital of New Hampshire has many points of historical interest. Notable is Strawbery Banke on the Piscataqua in downtown Portsmouth. This is the restoration of a complete maritime neighborhood of thirty buildings. On exhibit are the Captain John Clark house, 1750; the Governor Goodwin mansion, 1811; the Chase house, 1762; the oldest stud-framed dwelling in New Hampshire, the Sherburne house, 1695; Kingsbury house; the Dunaway store; and a boatshop of the 1790's in operation. Restoration is in progress on the surviving wing of the Provincial State House, circa 1757, on the Earl of Halifax and William Pitt Hotel where Washington spoke in 1789 and which Lafayette visited in 1782, and on other buildings. Nearby a number of early New Hampshire houses owned by various historical associations are open to the public. These include the Governor John Langdon mansion, the Moffat-Ladd house, the Wentworth-Coolidge mansion, and the John Paul Jones house.

Wolfeboro

The Libby Museum has a collection of Indian artifacts and mounted birds and animals in their natural settings. Only the cellar hole of the great house of Sir John Wentworth remains. The Clark house is shown by the Wolfeboro Historical Society.

Seasons of the year, days of the week, and hours of the day when these historic sites are open to the public—all subject to change—as well as directions for reaching them are to be found on the official New Hampshire tourist map. This is available from the New Hampshire Division of Economic Development, Concord, New Hampshire 03301.

Index

About the Author

James Playsted Wood has written a host of books and articles for both adults and young people, including Nelson's COLONIAL MASSACHUSETTS, THIS LITTLE PIG: The Story of Marketing, and EMILY ELIZABETH DICKINSON. He has ghosted speeches for public figures and his many published works include novels, short stories, biographies, histories, and verse. Besides his writing career he has taught at Amherst, done marketing research with Curtis Publishing Company, and been a member of the editorial staff of the *Journal of Marketing*. James Playsted Wood and his wife live in Springfield, Massachusetts.

Other Colonial Histories

COLONIAL GEORGIA, by Clifford Sheats Capps and Eugenia Burney

"Like its predecessors in the Colonial Histories series, this is an unusually readable history of the colony from prehistoric settlement through the Revolutionary War. The use of primary sources provides anecdotal immediacy without sacrificing continuity or pertinence, and the attractively arranged contemporary illusions sharpen the focus."

—*Kirkus Reviews*

COLONIAL MASSACHUSETTS, by James Playsted Wood

"Wood includes both the Plymouth and Massachusetts Bay settlements, pointing out differences and similarities in their backgrounds, development, and way of life. . . . The book contains numerous contemporary illustrations, photographs, a chronology, and a guide to historic sites."

—*ALA Booklist*

COLONIAL NEW JERSEY, by John T. Cunningham

"Highly interesting and factual presentation . . . of Colonial New Jersey from the first European encounter with the Lenni-Lenape Indians through the colony's role in the rebellion against England which led to the revolution."

—*Best Sellers*

COLONIAL NEW YORK, by Gardell Dano Christensen

"A vividly written, authoritative account. . . . The book's format is good, reproductions and illustrations are well chosen, and this title is an excellent choice for both school and public libraries."

—*School Library Journal*

COLONIAL PENNSYLVANIA, by Lucille Wallower

"This perceptive account of the founding of Pennsylvania utilizes primary sources for information and depicts objectively and sensitively the parts played by the Indians, Quakers, Moravians, and Mennonites. . . . This is the best book on the state for this age level."

—*School Library Journal* (Starred Review)

COLONIAL RHODE ISLAND, by Carleton Beals

"An exact—and exacting—history . . . that will be of great interest in the area and would, because of the import of the conflicts it conveys, the insights it purveys, be of value elsewhere—this, be it understood, chiefly on the high school level."

—*Kirkus Reviews*

COLONIAL SOUTH CAROLINA, by Eugenia Burney

"A very detailed anecdotal history . . . largely based on colonists' own journals and records. . . . The details presented, which are not found in most histories for children and young people, make this an excellent source for social studies units."

—*School Library Journal*

COLONIAL VIRGINIA, by Harold B. Gill, Jr. and Ann Finlayson

"Another volume in Nelson's interesting, solidly documented, attractively designed Colonial History series."

—*Kirkus Reviews*